Gilbert & Sullivan's
CHRISTMAS

Gilbert & Sullivan's
CHRISTMAS

compiled by

John Van der Kiste

SUTTON PUBLISHING

First published in the United Kingdom in 2000
Sutton Publishing Limited · Phoenix Mill · Thrupp
Stroud · Gloucestershire · GL5 2BU

British Library Cataloguing in Publication Data
A catalogue record for this book is available from the British Library.

ISBN 0-7509-2265-6

Typeset in 11/16.5 Sabon.
Typesetting and origination by
Sutton Publishing Limited.
Printed and bound in England by
J.H. Haynes & Co. Ltd, Sparkford.

Contents

Introduction: *Gilbert & Sullivan and Christmas*

John Van der Kiste

While they may not be associated with Christmas in the same way as their near-contemporary Charles Dickens, Gilbert & Sullivan have together and separately become part of the festive season. The former began his career as a dramatist through writing Christmas stories and pantomimes, while the latter's prolific output as a composer included music for several carols. Both were already successful in their chosen fields before they were initially brought together to collaborate on *Thespis*, a 'Christmas entertainment' for the 1871 season. Though only a modest success, it became the forerunner of the ever-popular 'Savoy operas', which dominated the English theatrical scene for the next two decades, played to packed audiences throughout Europe and America, and have remained firm favourites ever since.

William Schwenck Gilbert, born in November 1836, trained as a barrister but his heart lay in writing, initially humorous verse and stories, often illustrated with his own drawings. For a time he contributed to *Punch* and its shortlived, more anarchic rival *Fun*, several of his poems

W.S. Gilbert (By kind permission of Peter Joslin)

appearing under the pseudonym 'Bab', his childhood nickname. As a regular at the Arundel Club, The Strand, he knew the poets Dante Gabriel Rossetti and Algernon Charles Swinburne, both great admirers of his Bab Ballads. Another close friend was Tom Hood, editor of the journal *Saturday Night*, to which Gilbert was also a contributor. In 1865 both men wrote stories for a Christmas book, *A Bunch of Keys*, and similar Christmas annuals featuring their prose were published over the next four years. Gilbert continued to write and draw for other magazines including the *Cornhill, London Society*, and *Temple Bar*, as well as *Routledge's Christmas Annual*, 1867, and some of his stories contain the occasional Christmas element. 'Maxwell and I', published in another Christmas book *Rates and Taxes*, December 1866, and later in *Foggerty's Fairy and other tales*, 1892, is a semi-autobiographical tale of two playwrights which opens on the evening of the 25th as they are burning the midnight oil to complete a pantomime:

It was a dull Christmas night that Ted Maxwell and I were spending, boxed up in our chambers on a top-floor of Garden Court, Temple. Not but that we had plenty of friends in London whose merriment was tempered by the fact that circumstances beyond our control required that we should spend the afternoon and evening in chamber solitude. But that Grand Fairy Christmas Extravaganza, the One-Eyed Calendars, Sons of Kings; or, Zobeide and the Three Great Black Dogs, was due on the boards of a minor metropolitan theatre by ten o'clock on the following night, and there were two scenes still unfinished, and three or four songs still unwritten.

With hindsight this reveals that Gilbert had just discovered his true vocation as a writer for the theatre. Like many young dramatists more interested in earning a suitable income than aiming for the lofty ideals of high art, he had found an opening in Christmas pantomime – an entertainment defined in the Oxford English Dictionary as: 'a traditional theatrical performance, generally consisting of a dramatized fairy tale, with songs, dancing, topical jokes and conventional characters, usually performed in Britain around Christmas and the New Year season'. His first works for the stage were probably lyrics for Charles Millward's Christmas 1865 pantomimes, *King Salmon; or, Harlequin Prince Paragon and the Queen of the Valley of Perpetual Spring*, staged at the Theatre Royal, Liverpool; and *Cock-a-Doodle-Doo; or, Harlequin Prince Chanticleer and the Princess of the Golden Valley*, performed at Sadler's Wells. These were identical in many respects, written strictly to a formula, with plot outlines, some songs and dialogue common to both. In 1867 he wrote a complete pantomime in four days, *Harlequin Cock Robin and Jenny Wren; or, Fortunatus and the Water of Life, The Three Bears, The Three Gifts, The Three Wishes, and The Little Man Who Woo'd the Little Maid*. Including 'multiple ballets of flowers, canaries, and fish, a procession of birds, a march of bears, a double harlequinade, etc,' it earned him the sum of £60 from E.T. Smith, lessee and manager of the Lyceum Theatre. This experience gave the enterprising never-waste-anything wordsmith material for several articles over the next few years, among them 'Our Own Pantomime' in *Fun*, 11 January 1868, 'Getting Up a Pantomime' in *London Society* the same month, 'A Consistent Pantomime' in the *Graphic*, 16 January 1875, and 'My Pantomime' in the *Era Almanack*, 1884.

In August 1867 Gilbert married Lucy Agnes Turner. Although famous for his sharp tongue, his drill sergeant-like methods as a producer and director at rehearsals and a notorious refusal to suffer fools gladly, Gilbert was a devoted husband, and their marriage was childless but apparently happy. He and his wife loved having children around them, and he was a favourite uncle to the small sons and daughters of friends, giving them sweets and theatre boxes, and inviting them to parties. One of the latter included what was probably one of the first electrically lit Christmas trees in England, a natural development from some of the novel effects being pioneered on stage in their operas. At about the same time as he was unveiling this revolutionary manifestation of modern technology to awestruck youngsters, audiences flocking to *Iolanthe* at the Savoy Theatre were similarly wide-eyed at the sight of stars glittering from fairies' heads on which battery-operated lamps were switched on to help create an illusion of magic.

One of the first biographies of the writer, *W.S. Gilbert: his life and letters*, by Sidney Dark and Rowland Grey,

Sir Arthur Sullivan (By kind permission of Peter Joslin)

published in 1923, included extracts from a letter to the authors from Margery, daughter of the actor Cyril Maude, with whose family he and his wife were friends:

> Among my early recollections are those of receiving always at Christmas-time the most sumptuous and enormous box of chocolates from the then Mr. Gilbert. For which I used to write laboured little epistles of thanks in return on much decorated notepaper. I always signed it 'Your affectionate little friend, Margery Maude.' After one of these letters I received a lovely copy of the *Bab Ballads* inscribed to 'Miss Margery Maude, from her affectionate little friend, the Author.'

In 1869 he published a selection of *The Bab Ballads* in book form, and about a year later he first met the man with whose name his would be linked for ever after. Born in May 1842, by his mid-twenties Arthur Seymour Sullivan had composed symphonies, concertos, oratorios, hymns, songs, and the music for a comic opera in one act, *Cox and Box*, the libretto written by future *Punch* editor Francis Burnand. Gilbert and Sullivan were introduced by a mutual friend, the musician Frederick Clay, probably at a rehearsal for Gilbert's play *Ages Ago*, in the summer of 1870. Eighteen months later John Hollingshead, proprietor of the Gaiety Theatre, asked Gilbert to write the libretto of a comic opera for the Christmas season, and commissioned Sullivan to write the score. The result was *Thespis: or, The Gods Grown Old*.

After this Gilbert and Sullivan returned to their respective fields; the former had nearly thirty plays and libretti to his name, as well as several short stories and a considerable output of comic verse, while the latter continued composing music across a broad spectrum. Posterity is therefore indebted to the theatre owner and impresario Richard D'Oyly Carte, who reunited them three years later to collaborate on a one-act opera, *Trial by Jury*. It was so successful that the three men formed a business partnership resulting in ten more operas during the next fourteen years, namely *The Sorcerer* (first performed 1877), *HMS Pinafore* (1878), *The Pirates of Penzance* (1879), *Patience* (1881), *Iolanthe* (1882), *Princess Ida* (1884), *The Mikado* (1885), *Ruddigore* (1887), *The Yeomen of the Guard* (1888), and *The Gondoliers* (1889), collectively known as the Savoy Operas, after Carte's theatre in which most of them opened. (To be more accurate, the Savoy Operas include all those by various writers staged at the theatre in the late nineteenth century, though those not written jointly by Gilbert & Sullivan are little remembered today.) During this time they continued to write separately, but soon Victorian England could not think of one name without the other.

It was an often fractious relationship, for librettist and composer were very dissimilar in personality, professional partners who addressed each other by surname and whose respect for each other's abilities never ripened into genuine friendship. (Or, to quote from *HMS Pinafore* in what soon became a national catch-phrase, 'What, never?' 'Well –

The New Savoy Theatre, front towards the Thames Embankment. The original Savoy, built and opened in 1881 and the venue for every Gilbert & Sullivan collaboration from *Patience* onwards, was reconstructed and redecorated in 1929 (By kind permission of Mary Evans Picture Library)

hardly ever.') Upper-middle-class Gilbert was no socialist but he always maintained a gentle disrespect for pomposity and authority. With his humbler background the less abrasive Sullivan, a close friend of royalty and gentry, was regarded as something of a social climber by Gilbert. Sullivan's knighthood in 1883 made 'Mr Gilbert' more jealous than he would admit. The younger man thought his music for Gilbert's words somewhat beneath him, and

Richard d'Oyly Carte (the
D'Oyly Carte Archive)

yearned to concentrate on grand opera instead. In 1884 he considered dissolving the partnership, complaining that his tunes were in danger of becoming mere repetitions of his former pieces, and that 'the music is never allowed to rise and speak for itself', but he was persuaded to reconsider largely for motives of financial expediency rather than artistic integrity.

Not until the so-called 'carpet quarrel' during the spring of 1890, in which Gilbert argued with Carte for taking what he considered undue liberties on the financial side by apparently charging them for new front of house carpets at the Savoy Theatre, did the ever-widening fissure develop into an open breach. Sullivan sided with Carte, and for two years librettist and composer worked with other collaborators, but with only a fraction of their old success as a team. They buried the hatchet and wrote two further operas together, *Utopia Limited* (1893) and *The Grand Duke* (1896), but their day had been and gone, and neither achieved the popularity of their earlier joint efforts. They met for the last time at a revival of *The Sorcerer* in November 1898, which Carte had staged to commemorate its twenty-first anniversary. Though both men took their bows onstage at the end, they did not speak to each other and left the Savoy separately.

Racked by kidney trouble for years, Sullivan worked with other librettists on further operas for the Savoy and composed until shortly before his death from heart failure in November 1900. Gilbert likewise continued to write for the rest of his life, albeit less prolifically, and was knighted for services to the theatre in 1907. In May 1911 he succumbed to a heart attack while teaching friends to swim in the lake at his country house in Harrow, and rescuing one who had got into difficulties.

Christmas featured in several of Gilbert's writings, and Sullivan set a number of carols to music. However one would search in vain for festive references in most of their collaborations. Writing operas which could run for a year or more regardless of the season was far more profitable than 'Christmas entertainments' which would only last for a few weeks, and *Thespis* was the only one to make any substantial reference to the festive season.

The Sorcerer is the only other Gilbert & Sullivan opera to mention Christmas at all. In Act 1 John Wellington Wells describes his practice as a Sorcerer, or 'Necromancy in all its branches', and the most popular lines:

Our penny Curse – one of the cheapest things in the trade – is considered infallible. We have some very superior Blessings, too, but they're very little asked for. We've only sold one since Christmas – to a gentleman who bought it to send to his mother-in-law – but it turned out that he was afflicted in the head, and it's been returned on our hands. But our sale of penny Curses, especially on Saturday nights, is tremendous. We can't turn 'em out fast enough.

Dark and Grey commented on Gilbert's 'charming Lewis Carroll-like affection for girl-children', a substitute for the daughters he never had. A letter to a child, Miss Beatrice de Michele, written from his home The Boltons, South Kensington (13 December 1878), refers to the forthcoming festive season of which he would inevitably spend part in working:

. . . I am sorry you find it dull at Ramsgate. I can't understand it. Ramsgate in December ought to be only one remove from Paradise. But I say – Good God, how you will enjoy yourself when you come up to stop with us after Christmas. I can't understand your not enjoying Ramsgate. Do you bathe much? You used to be so fond of bathing – and I suppose the sands are not so crowded as they were in August, so you will not find the usual difficulty in getting a machine. Have you enjoyed many delightful sails in the shilling excursion yacht?

I can't tell you how I envy you at such a delightful place, and at such a delightful time of year. We poor creatures, who are obliged to spend Christmas in London, are really very much to be pitied . . .

Gilbert and his wife usually spent Christmas either entertaining children of friends, or else wintering abroad. One of his few surviving letters to mention the season was written to a cousin from his home at Grim's Dyke, Harrow (20 December 1910), at the start of what was to be his last Yuletide – a gloomy message with few tidings of comfort and joy:

> I received yesterday my diary for 1911, and as I looked through its blank pages it set me thinking. At my time of life (turned 74) the future becomes a serious consideration, and one can't help wondering what miseries, sorrows, calamities, deaths, and other horrors will have to be set down before it is finished – if ever it *is* finished, which seems unlikely. However, this train of thought is rather morbid and not in the least in keeping with the festive (?) season.

Yet it would be a mistake to read too much into this melancholy train of thought from a tired, elderly man who knew he did not have many more years, even months, ahead of him. Friends and contemporaries, such as Kate Terry Gielgud (see p. 140), have testified to his love of Christmas.

In his diaries Sullivan has left a clearer picture of how he spent Yuletide on various occasions. A workaholic who seemed intent on filling every waking hour possible with work, partly to distract himself from pain and increasing ill-health from his thirties onwards and partly to keep himself in the style to which he was accustomed – he was a heavy gambler – it was not unusual for him to spend at least part of the season in unremitting hard work.

Christmas 1875 found him in Glasgow, where he had gone to conduct concerts by the Glasgow Choral and Orchestral Union, and he celebrated Yuletide with Sir Coutts and Lady Caroline Blanche Elizabeth Lindsay at Balcarres, Colinsburgh, Fife, about 60 miles from Glasgow. A former Grenadier Guards officer, Sir Coutts was a patron of the arts, founder-proprietor of the Grosvenor Gallery, New Bond Street, where Rossetti and other pre-Raphaelites exhibited, and later the butt of Gilbert's 'Grosvenor Gallery, greenery-yallery' joke in *Patience*. Sullivan described the festivities in a letter to his mother, undated but presumably written at the end of December:

> Christmas day was beautiful and we had a tree in the afternoon for the servants. You have got a paper-knife off it, and Bertie [*his nephew, Frederick's third child Herbert, aged 7*] a top, Amy [*Frederick's eldest daughter, aged 12*] a thimble. . . . Yesterday Lindsay and I went for a long walk along the seashore. The view of the Firth of Forth at this moment is divine from my window. The sun, first red, then white, makes it look like a gold and silver sea alternately.

In December 1879 a 'Christmas version' of *HMS Pinafore* was produced at the Opera Comique, London, with matinee-only performances beginning during the Christmas holidays and running until March 1880. All parts were played by children aged from ten to thirteen, with the music rearranged for young voices. The dialogue, however, was not altered, incurring the wrath of Lewis Carroll who took offence at child actors playing the part of Captain Corcoran and saying, 'Damme, it's too bad!' on stage. Having been disappointed by his failure to persuade Sullivan to set some of his *Alice in Wonderland* songs to music for the theatre, Carroll was perhaps not unbiased.

Gilbert & Sullivan were in New York that Christmas, having sailed over some weeks earlier to supervise official productions of *HMS Pinafore* and begin secret rehearsals of *The Pirates of Penzance*. As copyright legislation in the United States was virtually non-existent, they were making no money from proliferating amateur productions of *Pinafore*, a situation they could hardly rectify without going there in person. By staging the premiere of *The Pirates* in New York, they hoped to lay claim to their copyright of the opera and defeat the 'pirate' productions. (The theme of piracy in their title was no coincidence.) In his haste Sullivan had left his draft of the score for Act 1 in England and he had to rewrite much of it from memory, and it was probably at Gilbert's suggestion that he reused 'Climbing over rocky mountain' from *Thespis*.

As the opera was due to open at the Fifth Avenue Theatre on 31 December, in order to meet the schedule

'The Children's *Pinafore*'. Christmas card, 1879.

for rehearsals he had to work every day throughout the festive week. On Christmas Day he worked solidly, dined with friends in the evening and then returned to his lodgings where he continued at his desk until 5.30 a.m. Barely pausing to sleep, he persevered with his labours all Boxing Day and supervised a rehearsal of Act 1 in the evening. On 27 December, the diary records: 'Finished full score at 7 a.m. on morning of 28th, Sunday.' Rehearsals occupied nearly every waking hour until the debut performance on New Year's Eve, and the final dress rehearsal ended at 1 a.m. on 30 December. Afterwards both men returned to Sullivan's lodgings with Frederick Clay and Alfred Cellier to put finishing touches to the overture. Clay, a musician and composer, is credited with having originally introduced the collaborators to each other, while Cellier had been a friend of the composer since they were choristers at the Chapel Royal, St James's. Sullivan and Cellier completed the composition and arrangement while the others copied the band parts, departing at 3 a.m. and leaving their colleagues to work for another two hours. Sullivan's diary for New Year's Eve notes that he 'got up feeling miserably ill, head on fire,' but got through the next few hours, fortified by twelve oysters and a glass of champagne. He finally climbed into bed at 3.30 a.m. on 1 January; 'felt utterly worn out.' Fortunately such endeavours brought their just reward, and the opera was an immediate success.

It is reassuring to read that he did relax during the next two festive seasons. By Christmas 1880 much of the next opera, *Patience*, had been written, but with no urgent deadline looming, he went to France. On Christmas Eve, while staying at the Hotel du Rhin in Paris, he visited his niece Amy at school, and after church on Christmas Day Amy and some of her friends from school came to see him. Twelve months later he was travelling even further south on holiday, across France by rail for Egypt. Crossing the Mediterranean on a French steamer with Port Said as his next destination, he recorded in his diary, 'thinking what a curious way it was of spending Christmas Day!'

During Christmas 1883 the recently knighted Sullivan was at his London home, 1 Queen's Mansions, Victoria Street, working on *Princess Ida*, and on the 25th he completed composing and writing out the score for a new quintet between midnight and 5 a.m. In the evening of 29 December he attended a pantomime, *Jack and Jill*, at the Surrey Theatre, came back to his house and 'finished scoring of opera (except 3 numbers to rewrite)' at 5 a.m. Next day he spent 'writing and scoring'. On 31 December he attended a rehearsal, wrote 'a new number', and spent part of the evening with friends, after which he returned to spend the rest of the night working at his desk, evidently well into the small hours, as his servants came to wish him a happy new year at midnight. There were some very long rehearsals during the next three days, full dress rehearsals lasting from 7 p.m. to 2 a.m. and 6.30 p.m. till 2.30 a.m. before first performance on 5 January 1884. He collapsed with pain later that morning, but a combination of injections of morphine to ease the pain, strong black coffee to keep him awake, and sheer will power helped him to come to the theatre to conduct the first night performance. 'Brilliant success. After the performance I turned very faint and could not stand.' He was put to bed in 'dreadful pain'. Ironically for all his efforts, *Ida* proved their least successful work of the 1880s, and in the wake of its successor, the ever-popular *Mikado*, it was all but forgotten.

At Christmas 1888 at his London home, Sullivan entertained guests and distributed gifts. Most of the company were friends of Fanny Ronalds; 'old Mr Carter', her father, two boxes of Villa Rothschild cigars; Mrs Carter silver scissors and a button-hook; Fanny herself 'eight pair –' (the dash is Sullivan's, obviously something personal); her son Reggie a cigar case, and her daughter Fanette two pairs of gloves. The servants were remembered, with gold cuff-links, cigar case, a gold chain and dressing gown for Louis, his gentleman, a boa (fur or leather collar), and a dress for the ladies respectively. Fanny Ronalds was his long-term mistress, amicably separated from her husband after eight years of marriage. Their relationship was readily tolerated by society; had she divorced her husband and remained with Sullivan either in or out of wedlock, he would have risked becoming a society outcast, and probably never have been knighted by the admiring Queen Victoria. New Year's Eve was spent at Mrs Ronalds' home, 7 Cadogan Place. At that time he had just finished working on incidental music for Henry Irving's production of *Macbeth*, which opened at the Lyceum Theatre on 29 December 1888; and *The Yeomen of the Guard*, which had opened in October, was playing to a packed house at the Savoy night after night. The first time Sullivan had seen the story of *Yeomen* was on Christmas Day 1887, which he had spent in bed, suffering agonies from a recurrence of his kidney problem. Gilbert and Carte had come to wish him the compliments of the season and show him the complete scenario, which he called 'a pretty story – no topsy-turvydom, very human and funny'.

Christmas 1889 was the last of Gilbert & Sullivan's golden age. *The Gondoliers*, their final undisputed success, had opened on 7 December. While Gilbert and

Inside the Savoy Theatre (showing the new electric lights) (The *Graphic*, 1881)

his wife were preparing to escape the winter of London in favour of four months abroad, principally in North Africa and India, Sullivan was still working hard. Another *Gondoliers* company had been assembled by Carte to perform in the United States; not a whole cast, but a group to provide reinforcement to the American performers engaged for the purpose, and Sullivan supervised a rehearsal at 10.45 a.m. on Christmas Day before returning home to work all afternoon. That evening he had a festive dinner with 'the folk of No. 7' and other guests. With Mrs Ronalds and other members of her family he went to pantomimes and other seasonal shows in London, including *Cinderella* at Her Majesty's Theatre on 27 December and on New Year's Eve, after attending the funeral at Westminster Abbey of the poet

Robert Browning in the morning, a mixed ballet-and-variety bill at the Alhambra including Marie Lloyd.

Three years later he celebrated the festive season in 1892 at Diodato, a villa at Cabbe-Roquebrune on the French Riviera. His friends Sir Charles and Lady Russell were also nearby, and a note to the latter, written on Boxing Day, suggests that something went seriously wrong with Christmas dinner, although it did nothing to dampen his spirits:

> Hot fomentations &c have restored my cook to good health and this morning she is desolée at yesterday's mishap. I had a dinner alone consisting of two cutlets and some cheese, and the turkey and plum pudding are awaiting your arrival. Will you come tonight or tomorrow whichever is most convenient? And will Sir Charles come and play his besique beforehand?

More than a hundred years later Gilbert & Sullivan's place as part of Britain's national heritage is assured, and their most famous works are still enjoyed the world over. In recent years enterprising Gilbert & Sullivan Societies in the United States have staged 'A Gilbert & Sullivan Christmas Carol', with the classic Dickens story set to the composer's music. As the novelist was a great admirer of Sullivan's work, and as Gilbert was a voracious reader of Dickens's stories, all three would surely have been amused at the idea of performers regaling today's audiences with such items as 'On a street in December, a little old man/Snapped

Sullivan's 'Grand National ballet' was first performed at the Alhambra Theatre, 25 May 1897. (Sir Arthur Sullivan Society)

"Bah humbug, bah humbug, bah humbug!", or 'Three little ghosts for Scrooge are we'. Moreover one can hardly consult a 'What's On' theatre programme from mid-November onwards without seeing at least one 'special Christmas season' series of performances of a specific opera, a 'Gilbert & Sullivan gala', or a 'seasonal selection of excerpts' drawn from the most popular.

Thespis

W.S. Gilbert

Thespis, *the first Gilbert and Sullivan collaboration, was their sole purpose-written Christmas entertainment. A two-act opera with a plot which involved switching the roles of mortals and ancient gods on Mount Olympus, it was written and rehearsed in a few weeks. As the audience expected elements of Christmas pantomime for their money, provision was made for a Transformation scene, and the appearance of a Harlequin and Clown. With Sullivan's brother Frederick playing Apollo, it was first staged on Boxing Day 1871 at the Gaiety Theatre, London. It suffered from poor preparation and lengthy hold-ups, and was hissed by some of the audience on its opening night when it ran an hour over time, leaving them 'in a fidgety state to get away' after midnight, but continued for 64 performances, until March 1872, considered a very good run for a piece provided expressly as an entertainment for Christmas. Though Gilbert later dismissed it as 'crude and ineffective', his libretto has survived, though not the score. Apparently dissatisfied with the music, Sullivan later went to great lengths to obtain all remaining copies from theatre manager, John Hollingshead, no doubt to destroy them. Only two songs remain; one, 'Little maid of Arcadee', was published separately, while another, 'Climbing over rocky mountain', was used in* The Pirates of Penzance. *The full opera has been revived on stage and recorded by amateur companies, featuring either a score adapted from Sullivan's other music or pastiche.*

A suite of Thespis ballet music, missing for over a century, was rediscovered in 1989 by two members of the Sir Arthur Sullivan Society. In Act 1, Mercury laments his role as the 'celestial drudge' and his subsequent life of petty crime, explaining why he has been so busy lately.

Mercury: Stealing on commission. There's a set of false teeth and a box of Life Pills for Jupiter – an invisible peruke and a bottle of hair dye – that's for Apollo – a respirator and a pair of galoshes – that's for Cupid – a full bottomed chignon, some auricomous fluid, a box of pearl-powder, a pot of rouge, and a hare's foot – that's for Venus.

Diana: Stealing. You ought to be ashamed of yourself.

Mercury: Oh, as the god of thieves I must do something to justify my position.

Diana and *Apollo* [contemptuously]: Your position.

Mercury: Oh, I know it's nothing to boast of even on earth. Up here, it's simply contemptible. Now that you gods are too old for your work, you've made me the miserable drudge of Olympus – groom, valet, postman, butler, commissionaire, maid of all work, parish beadle, and original dustman.

In this scene from *Thespis*, Thespis (J.L. Toole) agrees with Jupiter to exchange positions and let the aged gods visit earth for a year. Apollo (Frederick Sullivan, the composer's brother), Mars (Frank Wood), and Mercury (Nellie Farren) look on. (*Illustrated London News*, 6 January 1872)

Apollo: Your Christmas boxes ought to be something considerable.

Mercury: They ought to be but they're not. I'm treated abominably. I make everybody and I'm nobody. I go everywhere and I'm nowhere. I do everything and I'm nothing. I've made thunder for Jupiter, odes for Apollo, battles for Mars, and love for Venus. I've married couples for Hymen and six weeks afterwards, I've divorced them for Cupid, and in return I get all the kicks while they pocket the halfpence. And in compensation for robbing me of the halfpence in question, what have they done for me?

A little later in the libretto comes Thespis's song, assumed to be a gentle satire aimed at the Duke of Sutherland, renowned for his passion for driving trains. According to the Era, *the main theatrical newspaper of the time, J.L. Toole, playing the part of Thespis, brought the house down with this, and the* Pall Mall Gazette *commented that 'the orchestration is very novel, including, as it does, the employment of a railway bell, a railway whistle, and some new instrument of music imitating the agreeable sound of a train in motion'. If only Sullivan had not been at pains to deprive posterity of the chance to hear this song with the original music . . .*

I once knew a chap who discharged a function
On the North South East West Diddlesex Junction.
He was conspicuous exceeding,
For his affable ways, and his easy breeding.
Although a chairman of directors,
He was hand in glove with the ticket inspectors.
He tipped the guards with brand new fivers,
And sang little songs to the engine drivers.
'Twas told to me with great compunction,
By one who had discharged with unction
A chairman of directors function
On the North South East West Diddlesex Junction.
Fol diddle, lol diddle, lol lol lay.

Each Christmas day he gave each stoker
A silver shovel and a golden poker.
He'd buttonhole flowers for the ticket sorters
And rich Bath-buns for the outside porters.
He'd mount the clerks on his first-class hunters,
And he build little villas for the road-side shunters,
And if any were fond of pigeon shooting,

He'd ask them down to his place at Tooting.
'Twas told to me . . . etc.

In course of time there spread a rumour
That he did all this from a sense of humour.
So instead of signalling and stoking,
They gave themselves up to a course of joking.
Whenever they knew that he was riding,
They shunted his train on a lonely siding,
Or stopped all night in the middle of a tunnel,
On the plea that the boiler was a-coming
   through the funnel.
'Twas told to me . . . etc.

If he wished to go to Perth or Stirling,
His train through several counties whirling,
Would set him down in a fit of larking,
At four a.m. in the wilds of Barking.
This pleased his whim and seemed to strike it,
But the general public did not like it.
The receipts fell, after a few repeatings,
And he got it hot at the annual meetings.
'Twas told to me . . . etc.

He followed out his whim with vigour,
The shares went down to a nominal figure.
These are the sad results proceeding
From his affable ways and his easy breeding.
The line, with its rails and guards and peelers,

Was sold for a song to marine store dealers
The shareholders are all in the work'us,
And he sells pipe-lights in the Regent Circus.
'Twas told to me . . . etc.

It's very hard. As a man I am naturally of an easy disposition. As a manager, I am compelled to hold myself aloof, that my influence may not be deteriorated. As a man I am inclined to fraternize with the pauper – as a manager I am compelled to walk around like this: Don't know yah. Don't know yah. Don't know yah.
[Strides haughtily about the stage. Jupiter, Mars, and Apollo, in full Olympian costume appear on the three broken columns. Thespians scream]

Jupiter, Mars, Apollo: Presumptuous mortal.

Thespis: Don't know yah. Don't know yah.

Jupiter, Mars, Apollo [seated on broken pillars]: Presumptuous mortal.

Thespis: I do not know you. I do not know you.

Jupiter, Mars, Apollo: Presumptuous mortal.

Thespis: Remove this person.

[Stupidas and Preposteros seize Apollo and Mars]

Jupiter: Stop, you evidently don't know me. Allow me to offer you my card. *[Throws flash paper]*

Thespis: Ah yes, it's very pretty, but we don't want any at present. When we do our Christmas piece, I'll let you know. *[Changing his manner]* Look here, you know this is a private party and we haven't the pleasure of your acquaintance. There are a good many other mountains about, if you must have a mountain all to yourself. Don't make me let myself down before my company. *[Resuming]* Don't know yah, Don't know yah.

Christmas Sayings

In the same week that Thespis *opened at the Gaiety Theatre,* Punch *(30 December 1871) treated its readers to this gentle dose of festive superstition, 'Seasonable Folk-Lore'.*

It is considered very lucky, if on Christmas Eve the youngest child in the house finds under the doormat a Bank of England note.

It is unlucky to eat a mince-pie in the house of a Quaker, a prothonotary, a surrogate, a sinecurist, or a sworn Select vestryman.

If the sun shines on Christmas Day between eight and nine, there will be a considerable reduction in the Estimates; but if it snows, the Bank rate of discount will be raised during the next twelve months.

If you are a single man, fair, under six feet, and a good linguist, and will get out of bed between twelve and one on the morning of New Year's Day, and walk for two hours to and fro over London Bridge, with a crooked florin in your pocket, you will be sure to meet your future wife (should you marry again), at an evening party in the suburbs.

If the first thing you see when you come down-stairs on New Year's Day is a black cat, beware of crossing a bridge till the apples are in blossom; but if it is a gray horse, you may partake of pork pie without fear of consequences.

If a young unmarried woman eats three raisins running in a Christmas plum pudding which have not been stoned, and wishes three wishes while she looks over her left shoulder into the glass and throws a handful of mistletoe berries on a peat fire, without mentioning names or moving a muscle of her face, she must not be surprised, provided the wind is in the right quarter, if events happen as she desires.

The Children's Pinafore

A review simply signed 'C.S.' in the Theatre, *1 January 1880, bestowed high praise on the children's performance of* HMS Pinafore, *at the Opera Comique from December 1879 to March 1880 (see 'Gilbert & Sullivan and Christmas', p. 21). In view of the success of this and similar children's performances of* The Pirates of Penzance

during the 1884–85 season, one is tempted to wonder why none of the other operas was staged in similar fashion.
According to a review in the Examiner, *20 December 1879, nine-year-old Miss Effie Mason stole the show. 'She was the quaintest and funniest of little women, sang and acted with infinite humour, and when she bade the Captain confide in her because she was a mother, the audience literally choked with laughter.'*

Christmas treats to the little ones take various forms, and range from a Punch-and-Judy show in the back drawing-room to a visit to the far-famed and irresistible Polytechnic. But if anyone asked me how best I could delight a private box full of children of all ages and sizes, I should decidedly say by expending a little judicious capital at the Opéra Comique, where some exceedingly clever youngsters act 'H.M.S. Pinafore' in admirable style and without a tinge of juvenile precocity. There is nothing that children like better than to see children act. The Lilliputian scenes in the pantomime are always the most popular; and a manager has only to introduce a baby columbine, a youthful clown, and a boy pantaloon, to set the whole house in laughter. Recently . . . a capital pantomime was acted at the Adelphi entirely by masters and misses in their

Children's performances of *HMS Pinafore* and *The Pirates of Penzance* in New York were commemorated in a series of cards.

Whose praise Great Britain always chants,
And so do his cousins and his sisters and his aunts.'
Higgins' German Laundry Soap.

teens; and only last year we were all astonished with the sly fun and boundless vivacity of some Italian children, who played 'La Fille de Madame Angot'. But I don't believe that London has ever seen anything better than the baby 'Pinafore'. The humour is fresh and spontaneous, there is no parrot-like prating or tedious conceit, and, best or all, the children from first to last sing in tune. Where all are so good, thanks to clever Mr. Barker and Mr. Cellier, the instructor and conductor, it seems invidious to mention names; but the distinct enunciation and admirable clearness of Little Buttercup (Miss Effie Mason), who has a woman's voice with a child's face; the taste and modesty of the love-lorn Josephine (Miss Emilie Grattan); the quaint rollicking fun of Dick Deadeye (Master William Phillips), a most mischievous young rascal; and the clever imitations of the original Sir Joseph Porter and Captain Corcoran by Master Edward Pickering and Master Harry Grattan, deserve to be recognised. As for the Midshipmite, he creates a roar whenever he struts across the deck. But the thing that pleased me most was the singing and the sentimental acting of Master Harry Eversfield as Ralph Rackstraw. This boy has one of those pure and delicious cathedral voices that pierces the listener through and through; and be has acquired a wonderful style of singing for one so young. What a pity it seems that such a voice should ever break, possibly never to be recovered, haply to change into an uncertain baritone or a deep bass! The rest of the children treat the whole thing as a joke, but the heart of this lad is in his work; and it is a pleasure to watch his earnest and intelligent young face. It is worth all the money on the part of lovers of music to hear this boy sing Sullivan's music.

Getting Up A Pantomime

W.S. Gilbert

In this article published in London Society, *January 1868, illustrated with his own drawings. Gilbert took a detailed look at the seasonal entertainment of which he had become one of London's most renowned practitioners. Note particularly his gently self-deprecating observations in the last paragraph on the role of the author, himself 'by far the most unimportant of all his collaborateurs'.*

'HARLEQUIN, Columbine, Pantaloon, and Clown!' There is an agreeable magic in these words, although they carry us back to the most miserable period of our existence – early childhood. They stand out in our recollection vividly and distinctly, for they are associated with one of the very few real enjoyments permitted to us at that grim

stage of our development. It is a poetic fashion to look back with sentimental regret upon the days of early childhood, and to contrast the advantages of immaturity with the disadvantages of complete mental and physical efflorescence; but, like many other fashions – especially many poetic fashions – it lacks a solid substratum of common sense. The happiness of infancy lies in its total irresponsibility, its incapacity to distinguish between right and wrong, its general helplessness, its inability to argue rationally, and its having nothing whatever upon its half-born little mind, – privileges which are equally the property of an idiot in a lunatic asylum. In point of fact, a new-born baby is an absolute idiot; and as it reaches maturity by successive stages, so, by successive stages does its intelligence increase, until (somewhere about forty or fifty years after birth) it shakes off the attributes of the idiot altogether. It is really much more poetical, as well as much more accurate, to believe that we advance in happiness as our intellectual powers expand. It is true that maturity brings with it troubles to which infancy is a stranger; but, on the other hand, infancy has pains of its own which are probably as hard to bear as the ordinary disappointments of responsible men.

'Harlequin, Columbine, Clown, and Pantaloon!' Yes, they awaken, in *my* mind at all events, the only recollection of unmixed pleasure associated with early childhood. Those night expeditions to a mystic building, where incomprehensible beings of all descriptions held astounding revels, under circumstances which I never endeavoured to account for, were, to my infant mind, absolute realizations of a fairy mythology which I had almost incorporated with my religious faith. I had no idea, at that early age, of a Harlequin who spent the day hours in a pair of trousers and a bad hat; I had not attempted to realize a Clown with an ordinary complexion, and walking inoffensively down Bow Street in a cheap suit. I had not tried to grasp the possibility of a Pantaloon being actually a mild but slangy youth of two-and-twenty; nor had I a notion that a Columbine must pay her rent like an ordinary lodger, or take the matter-of-fact consequences of pecuniary unpunctuality. I believed in their existence, as I did in that of the Enchanter Humgruffin, Prince Poppet, King Hurly Burly, and Princess Prettitoes, and I looked upon the final metempsychosis of these individuals as a proper and legitimate reward for their several virtues and vices. To be a Harlequin or Columbine was the summit of earthly happiness to which a worthy man or woman could aspire, while the condition of Clown or Pantaloon was a fitting purgatory in which to expiate the guilty deeds of a life mis-spent. But as I grew older, I am afraid that I came to look upon the relative merits of those mystic personages in a different light. I came to regard the Clown as a good fellow whom it would be an honour to claim as an intimate companion; while the Harlequin degenerated into a rather tiresome muff, who delayed the fun while he danced in a meaningless way with a plain, stoutish person of mature age. As Christmases rolled by, I came to know some Clowns personally, and it interfered with my belief in them to find that they were not the inaccessible personages I had formerly supposed them to be. I was disgusted to find that they were, as a body, a humble and deferential class of men, who called me 'sir,' and accepted eleemosynary brandy and water with civil thanks: and when, at length, I was taken to a rehearsal of some 'Comic Scenes,' and found out how it was all done, my dim belief in the mystic nature of Pantomimists vanished altogether, and the recollection of what they had once been to me was the only agreeable association that I retained in connection with their professional existence.

But although familiarity with the inner life of a panto-mime may breed a certain contempt for the organized orgies of the 'Comic Scenes,' it cannot have the effect of rendering one indifferent to the curious people to whose combined exertion the institution owes its existence. They are, in many ways, a remarkable class of men and women, utterly distinct from the outside public in appearance, ways of thought, and habits of life. A fourth- or fifth-rate actor's conversation is perhaps more purely 'shoppy' than that of any other professional man;

his manner is more artificial, his dialogue more inflated, his metaphors more professional, and his appearance more eccentric. At the same time he is not necessarily more immoral or more improvident than his neighbours; and in acts of genuine, unaffected charity, he often sets an example that a bishop might imitate. There are good and bad people in every condition of life – and, if you are in a position to strike an average, you will probably find that the theatrical profession has its due share of both classes. Now for our Thumbnail Sketches.

The two poor old gentlemen who appear on the next page are 'supers' of the legitimate school. They are not of the class of 'butterfly-supers,' who take to the business at pantomime time, as a species of remunerative relaxation; they are at it, and they have been at it all the year round since their early boyhood. Their race is dying out now, for the degenerate taste of modern audiences insists on epicene crowds, and armies with back-hair and ear-rings. There was a goodly show of fine old regulation  'supers' at Astley's while 'Mazeppa' was being played a few weeks since; and I confess that the sight of the curious old banner-bearers in that extraordinary drama, had more interest for me than the developed charms of the 'beauteous Menkin.' The deportment of a legitimate 'super,' under circumstances of thrilling excitement, is a rich, and I am sorry to add, a rare study. Nothing moves him: his bosom is insensate alike to the dying throes of a miscreant and the agonized appeal of oppressed virtue; and he accepts the rather startling circumstance of a gentleman being bound for life to a maddened steed, as an ordinary incident of every-day occurrence – which, in point of fact, it is to him. He is a man of few – very few – words, and he gives unhesitating adherence to the most desperately perilous schemes with a simple 'We will!' – taking upon himself to answer for his companions, probably in consequence of a long familiarity with their acquiescent disposition. He is, in his way, an artist; he knows that an actor, however insignificant, should be close-shaved, and he has a poor opinion of any leading professional who sports an impertinent moustache. Mr. Macready was for years the god of his idolatry; and now that he is gone, Mr. Phelps reigns in his stead.

These two young ladies are to embody the hero and heroine of the piece. The taller one is Prince Poppet; the

shorter, Princess Prettitoes. The Prince will be redundant in back-hair, and exuberant in figure (for a prince); but he will realize many important advantages on his transformation to Harlequin, and a modification in the matters of figure and back-hair may count among the most important. 'Prince Poppet' is a bright, intelligent girl, and is always sure of a decent income. She sings a little, and dances a great deal, and can give a pun with proper point.

Her manner is perhaps just a trifle slangy, and her costume just a trifle showy, but her character is irreproachable. She is a good-humoured, hard-working, half-educated, lively girl, who gives trouble to no one. She is always 'perfect' in her words and 'business,' and being fond of her profession, she is not above 'acting at rehearsal,' a peculiarity which makes her an immense favourite with authors and stage-managers. The young lady, 'Princess Prettitoes,' who is talking to her, is simply a showy fool, intensely self-satisfied, extremely impertinent, and utterly incompetent. However, as a set-off to these drawbacks, she must be an admirable domestic economist, for she contrives to drive her brougham, and live en princesse, in a showy little cottage ornée, on three pounds a week. These young ladies are the curse of the stage. Their presence on it does not much matter, so long as they confine their theatrical talents to pantomime princesses; but they don't always stop there. They have a way of ingratiating themselves with managers and influential authors, and so it happens that they are not unfrequently to be found in prominent 'business' at leading theatres. They are the people who bring the actress's profession into contempt; who are quoted by virtuous but unwary outsiders as fair specimens of the ladies who people the stage. If these virtuous, but unwary outsiders, knew the bitter feeling of contempt with which these flaunting butterflies are regarded by the quiet, respectable girls who are forced into association with them, they would learn how little these people had in common with the average run of London actresses.

These two poor dismal, shivering women are 'extra ladies' – girls who are tagged on to the stock ballet of the theatre during the run of a 'heavy' piece. It is their duty while on the stage to keep themselves as much out of sight as they conveniently can, and generally to attract as little notice as possible until the 'transformation,' when they will

hang from the 'flies' in wires, or rise from the 'mazarin' through the stage, or be pushed on from the wings, in such a flood of lime-light that their physical deficiencies will pass unheeded in the general blaze. I believe it has never been satisfactorily determined how those poor girls earn their living during the nine months of non-pantomime.

Some of them, of course, get engagements in the ballets of country theatres, but the large majority of them appear to have no connection with the stage except at pantomime time. An immense crowd of these poor women spring up about a month or six weeks before Christmas, and besiege the managers of pantomime theatres with engagements that will, at best, provide them with ten or twelve shillings a week for two or three months; and out of this slender pay they have to find a variety of expensive stage necessaries. Many of them do needlework in the day-time, and during the 'waits' at night; but they can follow no other regular occupation, for their days are often required for morning performances. They are, as a body, a heavy, dull, civil, dirty set of girls, with plenty of good feeling for each other, and an overwhelming respect for the ballet-master.

This smart, confident, but discontented-looking man, with the air of a successful music-hall singer, is no less a personage than the Clown. His position is not altogether an enviable one, as pantomimes go, nowadays. It is true that he has the 'comic scenes' under his entire control; but comic scenes are no longer the important element in the evening's entertainment that they once were; and he is snubbed by the manager, ignored by the author, and inconsiderately pooh-poohed by the stage-manager. His scenes are pushed into a corner, and he and they are regarded as annoying and unremunerative impertinences to be cut off altogether as soon as the 'business' wanes. He undergoes the nightly annoyance of seeing the stalls rise and go out long before he

has got through his first scene. The attraction of a pantomime ends with the 'transformation,' and the scenes that follow are merely apologies for those that go before. The modern Clown is a dull and uninventive person: his attempts at innovation and improvement are limited to the introduction of dancing dogs, or a musical solo on an unlikely instrument. As far as the business proper of a Clown is concerned he treads feebly in the footsteps of his predecessors; and he fondly believes that the old, old tricks and the old, old catchwords have a perennial vitality of their own that can never fail. He is a dancer, a violinist, a stilt-walker, a posturist, a happy family exhibitor – anything but the rough-and-tumble Clown he ought to be. There are one or two exceptions to this rule – Mr. Boleno is one – but, as a rule, Clown is but a talking Harlequin.

This eccentric person on the chair is the Harlequin and ballet-master. He is superintending the developing powers

of his ballet, addressing them individually, as they go wrong, with a curious combination of flowers of speech, collecting terms of endearment and expressions of abuse into an oratorical bouquet, which is quite unique in its kind. He has the short, stubby moustache which seems to be almost peculiar to harlequins, and his cheeks have the hollowness of unhealthy exertion. He wears a practising dress, in order that he may be in a position to illustrate his instructions with greater precision, and also because he has been rehearsing the 'trips,' leaps, and tricks which he has to execute in the comic scenes. His life is not an easy one, for all the carpenters in the establishment are united in a conspiracy to let him break his neck in his leaps if he does not fee them liberally. He earns his living during the off-season by arranging ballets, teaching stage dancing, and, perhaps, by taking a music-hall engagement.

The gentleman in the initial is the Manager, who probably looks upon the pantomime he is about to produce as the only source of important profit that the year will bring him. Its duty is to recoup him for the losses attendant upon two or three trashy sensation plays, a feeble comedy, and a heavy Shakspearian revival; and if he only spends money enough upon its production, and particularly upon advertising it, he will probably find it will do all this, and leave him with a comfortable balance in hand on its withdrawal. He is a stern critic in his way, and his criticisms are based upon a strictly practical foundation – the question whether or not an actor or actress draws. He has a belief that champagne is the only wine that a gentleman may drink, and he drinks it all day long. He smokes very excellent cigars, wears heavy jewellery, drives a phaeton and pair, and is extremely popular with all the ladies on his establishment. He generally 'goes through the court' once a year, and the approach of this event is generally shadowed forth by an increased indulgence on his part in more than usually expensive brands of his favourite wine. He has no difficulty in getting credit; and he is surrounded by a troop of affable swells whom he generally addresses as 'dear old boys'.

The preceding sketch represents the 'property man' – an ingenious person whose duty it is to imitate everything in nature with a roll of canvas, a bundle of osiers, and half a dozen paint-pots. It is a peculiarity of most property men that they themselves look more like ingenious 'properties' than actual human beings; they are a silent, contemplative, pasty race, with so artificial an air about them that you would be hardly surprised to find that they admitted of being readily decapitated or bisected without suffering any material injury. A property man whose soul is in his business looks upon everything he comes across from his professional point of view; his only idea is – how it can best be imitated. He is an artist in his way; and if he has any genuine imitative talent about him he has plenty of opportunities of making it known.

This is the Author. I have kept him until the last, as he is by far the most unimportant of all his collaborateurs.

He writes simply to order, and his dialogue is framed upon the principle of telling as much as possible in the very fewest words. He is ready to bring in a 'front scene' wherever it may be wanted, and to find an excuse at the last moment for the introduction of any novelty in the shape of an 'effect' which any ingenious person may think fit to submit to the notice of the manager. From a literary point of view his work is hardly worth criticism, but he ought, nevertheless, to possess many important qualifications if it is to be properly done. It is not at all necessary that he should be familiar with the guiding rules of prosody or rhyme; nor is it required of him that he shall be a punster, or even a neat hand at a parody; but he must be quick at weaving a tale that shall involve a great many 'breeches parts.' He must be intimately acquainted with the details of stage mechanism, and of the general resources of the theatre for which he is writing. He must know all the catchy songs of the day, and he must exercise a judicious discrimination in selecting them. He must set aside anything in the shape of parental pride in his work, and he must be prepared to see it cut up and hacked about by the stage-manager without caring to expostulate. He must 'write up' this part and cut down that part at a moment's notice; and if one song won't do, he must be able to extemporize another at the prompter's table; in short, he must be prepared to give himself up, body and soul, for the time being, to manager, orchestra leader, ballet-master, stage-manager, scenic artist, machinist, costumier, and property-master – to do everything that he is told to do by all or any of these functionaries, and, finally, to be prepared to find his story characterized in the leading journals as of the usual incomprehensible description, and his dialogue as even inferior to the ordinary run of such productions.

A Consistent Pantomime

W.S. Gilbert

Gilbert returned to the subject of pantomime in an article in the
Graphic, *16 January 1875. This was part short-story and part*
memoir; his 'dear little boy' referred to in the first two paragraphs is
pure artistic licence, as was perhaps his reference to appearing on
stage as a clown at the age of three.

My family is, and has been, for many years under a
Curse, and the terms of the curse are that every male
member of my family must be a clown. A member of my
family cannot avoid his Destiny. He may hope to do so by

entering the Navy before the
mast, or by reading for holy
orders, or by driving a loco-
motive, or what not, but sooner
or later he is sure to find himself slowly drifting into the
troubled waters of Pantomime.
Indeed, my family has become
so convinced of this, that it
never occurs to us to turn our thoughts to any other line
of business. When I was three years old I appeared as an
infant clown; and my dear little boy, who will be three
next Christmas, will make his debût under similar
circumstances. If I had twenty little boys, I should make

clowns of them all, because I feel that it would be waste of time and money to apprentice them to any other calling. So I bow to fate and do all that in me lies to make the best of a bad job. My dear little boy is getting on nicely – he is already a very fair rough-and-tumble clown, and will make a great sensation, I am convinced, when he appears next year. I don't train him with dummies – I train him with the real thing. I have taught him to affect extreme terror whenever he meets a policeman in the street, and when I go shopping, I take him with me, and he slaps the door-post as a matter of course, and then lies down across the entry as I do in my comic scenes. I have also taught him to propose marriage to all the young ladies he meets, and it is amusing to remark their good-humoured surprise when the little fellow throws himself at their feet, exclaiming 'I loves yer to substraction!'

My friend Billy Shivers, the Fire Monarch from Cremorne, has lent me a pair of asbestos trousers, which enables my dear little boy to play with my calves with a real hot poker. He has not yet sufficient length of arm to make a good butter slide, but, with the commonest Dorset as high as thirteen pence, this does not so much matter. Besides, for a real butter slide you want good firm fresh butter that you can grip, and that will resist the

warmth and pressure of the fingers for half a minute, and this can't be obtained under twenty pence, which is out of the question. The oddest part of the thing is that the dear little fellow has no idea that, in behaving as I have taught him to behave, he is doing anything unusual. He is too young to understand that he is merely learning a profession; he believes that he is receiving the ordinary education of a young English gentleman. As soon as he is old enough to understand me, I shall, of course, explain to him that nobody has any real reason to be afraid of a policeman, and that, unless his friends happen to wear asbestos trousers, he will not be expected to rub red-hot pokers against their legs.

I am a person of some education, and (I hope) refinement of thought. I cannot say I have much respect for my profession, but, as I am compelled to follow it, I am naturally anxious to see it elevated in popular estimation. I have studied the Greek drama in its native form, and I am familiar with the principles upon which the classic French plays were constructed. I do not express an unqualified approval of the Unities, for I consider that dramatic interest, probability, and the natural sequence of events, well and good, but if they can't, let them go overboard. It will be seen from this that I cannot be charged with any bigoted adherence to archaic postulates. I take a reasonable and large-minded view of these matters that will secure the sympathy and concurrence of all enlightened playgoers.

In my zeal for my particular branch of the profession I have often spent days and nights for many weary weeks at a time in constructing theories that will reconcile the inconsistencies of the comic scenes of a pantomime. I have gone back to the old Italian stage to see if I could discover any reason why a clown who blows a policeman out of a thirty-two pounder should be held by passers-by to have done an everyday thing that scarcely calls for comment. But I can find nothing in old Italian pantomime to justify this. Indeed, the policeman has no definite existence, as a policeman, in old Italian pantomime. He is an excrescence of recent growth, and his intrusion should be regulated by those rules of common sense which are rigorously applied to all other forms of dramatic composition.

A clown's career, as represented on the stage, is one unchequered course of triumphant villainy. His every wish is gratified at once – every imposition that he practices is absurdly successful – he robs, assaults, and murders with monstrous impunity. If he is baulked at any stage of his misdoings, it is only that his final triumph may be made the more effective. If he so steals that he is detected and collared, it is that  he may do to his captors that which will make them wish they had never collared him. In fact, he is a Tartar, and the triumph of those who catch him is short indeed.

Now, how much more dramatically effective it would be if this immunity from all the consequences of his crimes were done away with, and how fruitful of results his merest misdeeds would become! We will suppose that Clown steals a baby from a perambulator driven by a nurse girl whose attention is distracted by the conversation of a soldier. This is a good dramatic incident in itself, and probability is in no way violated. The nurse girl, unconscious of her loss, drives away the empty perambulator, and Clown is left alone with the baby. He fondles it, addresses it in the ridiculous language of the nursery, and eventually, procuring a bowl of soft food (conveniently labelled 'PAP' by some methodical mother, whose china closet must present a curious aspect, if all the other vessels are similarly distinguished), proceeds to feed it in the usual manner. He sits down on the stage with the baby in his lap (a ventriloquial baby whose cries come from behind the scenes) and the bowl at his side. He takes a spoonful of pap, tastes it, finds it too hot, splutters, tries again, finds that it will do very well, and pops it into the infant's mouth, carefully scraping up the liquor which is supposed to have trickled from the baby's lips on to its dress, and pouring it down the child's throat, finishing by 'spatting' its face with the bowl of the spoon before sitting upon it and crushing it utterly. Now so far the dramatic conception of the 'business' is admirable. Allowing for a certain spice of pantomimic exaggeration, there is nothing done that, under the circumstances, might not have been reasonably expected. Given a savage, painted, grotesque barbarian, heartless and vicious, but with a fund of coarse imitative humour which helps to tone down the horror that his infamous deeds would certainly engender, there is nothing in this recital of events to militate, in any way, against probability. But what does the Clown do with the poor crushed corpse of his innocent little victim? Does he attempt to conceal the traces of his appalling crime? No. He seizes the poor little broken flower by the legs and slaps the pantaloon's face with its head. It is then cast aside altogether, the attention of the murderer is directed to another matter, and of the baby's death nothing more is heard or seen. It has no bearing on the story, it is simply lugged in, neck and crop, and abandoned as soon as it has served its end: having excited the interest of the audience by presenting to them an atrocious murder committed by a quaint savage on a helpless infant, the author turns abruptly to another matter which in its turn is abandoned when it has served the ephemeral purpose of the moment.

Now this may be Pantomime, but certainly is not Art. It is one of the canons of Art, as applied to dramatic matters that if you excite an interest you are bound to allay it, and the policy of this maxim will be quite evident if we follow out the events that should result from this atrocious child murder in their regular sequence.

We will suppose that the Clown has committed the murder, and he and Pantaloon, miserable and panic stricken, are in momentary dread of arrest. Here is a fine opportunity for a clown, who is also an actor. I would have him exaggerate his terror, because he has to make it comic as well as fearful – it should be broadly grotesque, but still as true to nature as is compatible with caricature. Above all things, he should seem to believe in the terror he is expressing, and this can never be the case as long as he is shielded by a Clown's conventional immunity from consequences. What has such a protected Clown to fear? As well might Achilles dread a spear-thrust at his breast. No; if the Clown's part is to be a good acting part he must be prepared to take the legitimate consequences of his acts; and with those in view he will be as terrified as you or I should be, and express his terror in much more vivid colours. Let him gape and shiver, let his eyes start, and his head sink into his chest, let his knees shake, and let him roar with apprehension. The Pantaloon's terror, that of a doddering old reprobate, should, of course, contrast with the vigorous emotion of his robust companion.

Well, Justice is on their track, and a policeman arrests them at last (and here the Clown may double up the Policeman if he will – he may even cut him in two, but if he does he will surely be tried for that murder also), Clown and Pantaloon, after a desperate resistance on the part of the former, are safely lodged in jail, where they may run

riot among the cells, and play the mischief with all the prisoners. A 'front scene' may follow, representing Clown and Pantaloon's interview with their attorney – and here Clown may make it as hot for the lawyer as he likes, but he must be sure to allow his annoyances to spring from palpable boorish awkwardness, and not from an intention to annoy a gentleman upon whose good favour his life may, in a measure, depend. At the same time, Clown may be reasonably supposed to have recovered in some degree from his depression, and elated by the servile lawyer's assurances that he has nothing to fear, he may bonnet the warders or play any other practical joke upon them that may occur to him.

It would be tedious to follow our Clown's course of action in detail. The trial scene would, of course, be his pièce de résistance, and here his old terror, mingling with his keen sense of the absurdity of entrusting a man's fate to the decision of twelve men picked from the most ignorant, narrow-minded, opinionated, intolerant, and dishonest class of beings in London, will afford a clown-actor another opportunity of rescuing his rôle from the contempt into which he has fallen. Harlequin, too, might produce grand effects with his wand in this scene – irritating the counsel for the prosecution by causing the jury to disappear and reappear in another part of the court, and further complicating matters by causing the judge on the bench to change places with the prisoner in the dock. He might cover the judge with confusion by causing annoying placards to appear on the walls, such as, 'This gentleman was raised to the Bench for voting with his Party,' or by hanging inscriptions on the necks of the jury, describing the various adulterations they habitually introduce into the wares in which they deal. The Clown would of course conduct his own defence, and an evident

I WAS MADE A JUDGE FOR VOTING WITH MY PARTY.

assumption of bravado on his part, struggling with his sense of abject terror as the damning facts of his crime are brought one by one before the eyes of the court, would give an emotional actor a further chance of distinguishing himself. Of course the scene would conclude with a verdict of Guilty, and a solemn sentence of Death, but at this point, I am afraid, the Presiding Genius of the opening scenes must interfere in order to end the play in the usual fashion, though the private execution of Clown and Pantaloon before the prison authorities and members of the Press would be a most effective moral finale if the audience would put up with it.

I think I have said enough to show that there is no reason why the part of Clown should be confined to acrobats and mummers. If the rôle be treated as I propose it would become the focus towards which the ambition of every distinguished actor might tend. Let Mr. Irving or Mr. Phelps courageously take the part by the hand and give it the stamp of respectability, and there will not be an emotional actor in the profession who will not burn to play it. And if this communication should have the effect of bringing about this result I shall not have written in vain.

The Gibeonites of the Stage

C.H. d'E. Leppington

A more down-to-earth view of working conditions for the performers is to be found in this extract from an article published in the National Review, *1891. The Gibeonites were Biblical 'hewers of wood and drawers of water' (Joshua 9:29).*

A pantomime generally lasts from two to three months, but performers are engaged for a certain number of weeks 'and the run', that is to say, for as much longer as it may answer to keep the piece before the public. A week or two's notice is given if the pantomime has to be withdrawn sooner.

The pantomime season opens on Boxing night, but daily rehearsals will have been going on for three to six weeks previously. The performers are paid for their attendance during the last week (sometimes the last fortnight) of the rehearsal. It is no easy task to drill a troop of perhaps two or three score of youngsters (some stupid, some recalcitrant, and the bulk of them just about the age described in *Tom Brown* as the most mischievous of British boyhood) to a faultless performance of long-continued concerted action; and as the weeks fly past, and the spectre of the opening night looms nearer and nearer, rehearsals follow quicker and last longer, till (to quote one case I heard of) the troupe is summoned for four o'clock on Christmas Eve, and kept at it for the next twelve hours straight off, in view of opening on Boxing Night.

Christmas Bab Ballads

W.S. Gilbert

Gilbert published his first selection of Bab Ballads *in book form in 1869. These had previously appeared in* Fun *or occasionally* Punch. *In a critical moment he said that they were 'composed hastily, and under the discomforting necessity of having to turn out a quantity of lively verse on a certain day in each week.' The two following ballads, first published in* Fun, *on 6 January 1866 and 28 December 1867 respectively, have Christmas themes.*

Ballad: The Phantom Curate. A Fable

A BISHOP once – I will not name his see –
Annoyed his clergy in the mode conventional;
From pulpit shackles never set them free,
And found a sin where sin was unintentional.
All pleasures ended in abuse auricular –
The Bishop was so terribly particular.
Though, on the whole, a wise and upright man,
He sought to make of human pleasures clearances;
And form his priests on that much-lauded plan
Which pays undue attention to appearances.

He couldn't do good deeds without a psalm in 'em,
Although, in truth, he bore away the palm in 'em.

Enraged to find a deacon at a dance,
Or catch a curate at some mild frivolity,
He sought by open censure to enhance
Their dread of joining harmless social jollity.
Yet he enjoyed (a fact of notoriety)
The ordinary pleasures of society.

One evening, sitting at a pantomime
(Forbidden treat to those who stood in fear of him),
Roaring at jokes, SANS metre, sense, or rhyme,
He turned, and saw immediately in rear of him,
His peace of mind upsetting, and annoying it,
A curate, also heartily enjoying it.

Again, 'twas Christmas Eve, and to enhance
His children's pleasure in their harmless rollicking,
He, like a good old fellow, stood to dance;
When something checked the current of his frolicking:
That curate, with a maid he treated lover-ly,
Stood up and figured with him in the 'Coverley!'

Once, yielding to an universal choice
(The company's demand was an emphatic one,
For the old Bishop had a glorious voice),
In a quartet he joined – an operatic one.
Harmless enough, though ne'er a word of grace in it,
When, lo! that curate came and took the bass in it!

One day, when passing through a quiet street,
He stopped awhile and joined a Punch's gathering;
And chuckled more than solemn folk think meet,
To see that gentleman his Judy lathering;
And heard, as Punch was being treated penally,
That phantom curate laughing all hyaenally.

Now at a picnic, 'mid fair golden curls,
Bright eyes, straw hats, BOTTINES that fit amazingly,
A croquet-bout is planned by all the girls;
And he, consenting, speaks of croquet praisingly;
But suddenly declines to play at all in it –
The curate fiend has come to take a ball in it!

Next, when at quiet sea-side village, freed
From cares episcopal and ties monarchical,
He grows his beard, and smokes his fragrant weed,
In manner anything but hierarchical –
He sees – and fixes an unearthly stare on it –
That curate's face, with half a yard of hair on it!

At length he gave a charge, and spake this word:
'Vicars, your curates to enjoyment urge ye may;
To check their harmless pleasuring's absurd;
What laymen do without reproach, my clergy may.'
He spake, and lo! at this concluding word of him,
The curate vanished – no one since has heard of him.

Ballad: At a Pantomime. By a Bilious One

An Actor sits in doubtful gloom,
His stock-in-trade unfurled,
In a damp funereal dressing-room
In the Theatre Royal, World.

He comes to town at Christmas-time,
And braves its icy breath,
To play in that favourite pantomime,
HARLEQUIN LIFE AND DEATH.

A hoary flowing wig his weird
Unearthly cranium caps,
He hangs a long benevolent beard
On a pair of empty chaps.

To smooth his ghastly features down
The actor's art he cribs, –
A long and a flowing padded gown.
Bedecks his rattling ribs.
He cries, 'Go on – begin, begin!
Turn on the light of lime –
I'm dressed for jolly Old Christmas, in
A favourite pantomime!'
The curtain's up – the stage all black –
Time and the year nigh sped –
Time as an advertising quack –
The Old Year nearly dead.

The wand of Time is waved, and lo!
Revealed Old Christmas stands,
And little children chuckle and crow,
And laugh and clap their hands.

The cruel old scoundrel brightens up
At the death of the Olden Year,
And he waves a gorgeous golden cup,
And bids the world good cheer.

The little ones hail the festive King, –
No thought can make them sad.
Their laughter comes with a sounding ring,
They clap and crow like mad!

They only see in the humbug old
A holiday every year,
And handsome gifts, and joys untold,
And unaccustomed cheer.
The old ones, palsied, blear, and hoar,
Their breasts in anguish beat –
They've seen him seventy times before,
How well they know the cheat!

They've seen that ghastly pantomime,
They've felt its blighting breath,
They know that rollicking Christmas-time
Meant Cold and Want and Death, –

Starvation – Poor Law Union fare –
And deadly cramps and chills,
And illness – illness everywhere,
And crime, and Christmas bills.

They know Old Christmas well, I ween,
Those men of ripened age;
They've often, often, often seen
That Actor off the stage!

They see in his gay rotundity
A clumsy stuffed-out dress –
They see in the cup he waves on high
A tinselled emptiness.

Those aged men so lean and wan,
They've seen it all before,
They know they'll see the charlatan
But twice or three times more.
And so they bear with dance and song,
And crimson foil and green,
They wearily sit, and grimly long
For the Transformation Scene.

A later collection, Songs of a Savoyard *(1890), contained
the following rather misogynistic verse, again with a small
festive allusion.*

Ballad: Her Terms

My wedded life
Must every pleasure bring
On scale extensive!
If I'm your wife
I must have everything
That's most expensive –
A lady's-maid –
(My hair alone to do
I am not able) –
And I'm afraid
I've been accustomed to
A first-rate table.
These things one must consider when one marries –
And everything I wear must come from Paris!
Oh, think of that!
Oh, think of that!
I can't wear anything that's not from Paris!
From top to toes
Quite Frenchified I am,
If you examine.
And then – who knows? –
Perhaps some day a fam –
Perhaps a famine!
My argument's correct, if you examine,
What should we do, if there should come a f-famine!

Though in green pea
Yourself you needn't stint

In July sunny,
In Januaree
It really costs a mint –
A mint of money!
No lamb for us –
House lamb at Christmas sells
At prices handsome:
Asparagus,
In winter, parallels
A Monarch's ransom:
When purse to bread and butter barely reaches,
What is your wife to do for hot-house peaches?
Ah! tell me that!
Ah! tell me that!
What IS your wife to do for hot-house peaches?
Your heart and hand
Though at my feet you lay,
All others scorning!
As matters stand,
There's nothing now to say
Except – good morning!
Though virtue be a husband's best adorning,
That won't pay rates and taxes – so, good morning!

The Mask-Maker

Alfred Thompson

This extract comes from an article in the Mask, 1868, *a journal published and mostly written by Alfred Thompson.*

Ah! But it is at Christmas time that the greatest exhibition of my industry and ability takes place. Getting up the pantomime is the thing to bring out your capacity, and to prove whether you are really a man of genius or an impostor. Well do I remember one particular pantomime we had at our house. It was called Polly Put the Kettle On; or, Harlequin King Cricket, the Demon of the Red-Hot Poker; and the Fairy of the Enchanted Hearthstone. It was a very heavy production for the property department, for it was full of properties, and the management was very late with it. When our stage-manager, Mr Pincher, issued to me 'my plot', by which I refer to the list of things I had got to make for the pantomime, and only about three weeks to do it in, I must say that even I, accustomed as I had been to works of a gigantic character, I just say even I staggered – although never given to drink – like an intoxicated carpenter. It was all written out on long slips of paper, like the bill of fare at the coffee shop where, in the slack season, I take my meals; and the list, in its entire length, measured exactly seven yards. I hung it up in my room, and sat down, and contemplated it in speechless amazement.

The first item on my programme was as follows:

1st scene, Demon Cave
It was in this scene that the Demon revel took place, followed by the sudden appearance of the Demon King in his car, who, after consulting the magic cauldron, despatched the Red-hot Poker to earth by a favourite sprite. This was the list of things I had to make:–

Twelve demons' heads; ditto three-pronged spears; ditto wings; ditto tails; and one dragon to vomit fire, with tail to move. One cauldron, to burn blue; demon king's head; one red-hot poker; four owls, with lighted eyes, to change to green imps; twelve squibs, to light on demons' tails; red fire; head to fit Mr Gruffs.

And here I may observe that there is nothing like demons in a pantomime. They make a great mistake when they cut out the demons. Nothing like the smell of lots of squibs and red fire early in the evening. It's more fragrant to the children than Rimmel's perfume. It's true it makes the old people choke; but don't it recall to them the memories of their youthful days, and what can be more interesting?

The next scene in the pantomime was of course the Fairy Scene. A gorgeous affair, painted by Young Skipper, and here, of course, the Ballet, by the young ladies, took place, followed by the appearance of the Fairy Queen, who determined to protect the lovers, and having summoned some Christmas properties as indications of the season, another short ballet took place, and the scene closed on Tableau. This was on my list:–

2nd Scene – Fairy Scene.

Twenty-four silver helmets for ballet, eight superior, twenty-four javelins for ditto, eight superior; twenty-four shields, eight superior; twenty-four garlands of flowers, eight superior; twenty-four tails of false hair, eight very superior; a cupid's bow and arrows; one dove to fly off; one plum-pudding to walk; one wedding-cake to walk; one round of roast beef to sing and dance, white fire.

I have ever felt great pride in being called upon to contribute to the proper turning-out of our young ladies, only I could never understand why Mons. Anatole, our ballet master, always showed such a determination to make them carry heavy properties while they were dancing. It is not pleasant to have to dance with a quantity of implements in your hands, and it was always very distracting to myself, for it is difficult to make twenty-four giddy young creatures, eight, however, superior, understand where their properties are, and then to get them to take on the right ones. Over the eight superior I always took great pains. These were for our eight leading young ladies, who did all the dancing in the front, and who were handsome young ladies, and very beautifully formed, and who, in the ballet, completely shut out all the other young ladies who couldn't dance over much, but who made tremendous pretence at the back that they were accomplished performers, which altogether, gave a liveliness to the scene, and made the audience think that they were all superior young ladies, instead of there being only eight worthy of the designation.

The Hive of Pantomime

'Feraldt'

A decade later 'Feraldt' added his comments in these extracts from an article in the Theatre, *January 1880.*

'Perhaps you would be good enough to come down to the rooms and see if you are satisfied with the ballets – Signor Bacolo has completed the first, and thinks the second is just what you would like.'

'All right. I'll be there at eleven sharp.'

We are getting near Christmas, and have only another fortnight to complete everything connected with the 'Gorgeous Original Christmas Pantomime, entitled Harlequin Ali Baba and the Wonderful Lamp, or the Wizard Bluebeard and the Little Fairy Cinderella' – (I may say by way of parenthesis I detest this mixture of simple fairy stories, and should never think of muddling young heads with such a tissue of complicated incidents; but the title is only imaginary, and will do as well as any other) – a pantomime which is to eclipse, we hope, everything yet seen in fun, beauty, and all the rest of it.

People who take their children to pantomimes have little or no idea of the time, thought, and labour it takes to put on to the stage of one of these elaborate entertainments. A manager who looks after the production of pieces he brings out in his own theatre must be everywhere and everything at once. He may have the best coadjutors, the cleverest master-carpenter, the most artistic scene-painter, a genius as a property-man, and an experienced author whose work is interpreted by the best available talent; but if he does not give an eye to all departments there will be hitches too evident, and mistakes too palpable, which only the good-humoured criticism of Christmas will overlook.

'Let me see, that ballet-master wants me at eleven. Send for Mr Ossidew (the property-man) and Mr Rowe Spink (the scenic artist). Oh, here is Mrs Tarlatan, the wardrobe-mistress. Well, have all the costumes arrived?'

'Good-morning, sir. There's three cases arrived from Arisso's, which I've opened. All the principals except the king's boots and the princess's hat and feathers. They say the twelve pages is there, but I only count eleven. They look splendid, sir, and I should like you to see 'em.'

'I'll come up to the wardrobe at two without fail. How about the demon ballet?'

'There is only half of 'em come, and the tights ain't finished yet. But they've promised them by next Thursday.'

'Dear, dear! that's very late! Any boots arrived?'

'Not likely, sir. Them's always the last. Cavis makes first-rate boots, but he do make one nervous at the end.'

Here the master-carpenter enters, and Mrs Tarlatan retires. The master-carpenter, who always looks like a general officer with a grievance, has come to say that the scene-rehearsal will be ready at midnight as soon as the usual night performance has been disposed of. Also: 'Mr Appythort, the hauthor, wants a new trap for the demon queen's first entrance. We shall have to cut away a lot of joists, and might as well use the bridge in the third entrance.'

I run up with Mortice at once and inspect the stage – the trap can easily be made, and two men are put on to it at once. The spirits of the demon queen and the author's will both rise on the opening night to their individual satisfaction.

'Ah, Mr Rowe Spink, I hope I haven't taken you away from your work?'

'Not at all, sir. I was coming down to ask you if it would not be better to add another border in the palace scene. You'll see tonight. Mortice thinks we can do without it. By the way, Mr Irons will be here tomorrow to try the transformation.'

'So much the better. Where's Haresfoote? Oh, Mr Haresfoote (the stage-manager), mind all the ballet-ladies and the extras are here tomorrow night for the transformation scene.'

'The extras are not all chosen yet, sir. I've got thirty or forty girls waiting now in the hall to be selected when you are at liberty.'

'Very well, I'll come at once. I shall come up to the paint-room, Mr Spink, this afternoon, and – ah, you're here, Ossidew. How are the properties getting on? Is the practicable cannon ready?'

'All right, sir; everything will be there by the opening-night.'

Now there is no more fatal rock than this behind the scenes. 'All right' on the opening night generally means all wrong. If a man tells me a dress or a property, or, if it comes to that, a part will be all right on the opening-night, I say it will be all wrong, and must be specially provided for. Of course, when I get up to the property-room, the practicable cannon, out of which a whole regiment of small soldiers is going to be shot, apparently into space, is not commenced.

'What do you think of them heads, sir?' says Mr Ossidew, when he has been sufficiently lectured on the necessity of being beforehand with all his productions. 'They wants just a little bit of hartistic treatment to be first-rate.' The heads are enormous papier-mâché (or 'paper-mash', as Ossidew calls it) effigies to be worn by the king's body-guard; and the supers who have been recruited for their particular regiments may be heard on the stage below stamping about under the drilling of the stage-manager, Mr Haresfoote. I can hear him coming up from beneath me like the ventriloquist's 'man in the cellar', a voice shouting 'Confound it all! How many more times are we to do this over again? Didn't I say, after crossing the bridge and coming down the rake, you are to march two and two down to the centre of the footlights, where you see the conductor in the orchestra, and then, half turning right and half left, you will circle round into the places I showed you? Now then, pay attention! We can't stay all day at this!' But to return to the properties. The heads are all waiting to be painted and varnished; the armour is being cleaned up; the comic halberds are being fixed; the banners are all arriving at completion, and the property horses and wolves (there is a comic scene recalling the thrilling ride of Mazeppa) *[a dramatization based on a poem by Byron, in which the heroine is tied to the back of a horse and chased across spectacular mountain scenery by a pack of wolves]* are being tried by some of the property-men to see if they will work their tails and roll their eyes with some semblance of reality. Everything seems tolerably forward, and after repressing Ossidew's desire to make all the hand-properties – that is, the accessories carried by ballet-girls, such as wreaths, torches, or assegais – twice as large and three times as heavy as is necessary, I again return to the stage, which I now find swarming with boys who are to be drilled into an attack on some ogre's castle or who represent imps and tadpoles in the opening. . . . The boys are using their swords and guns for the first time today, and well they take to them. Meanwhile I must go and select the extras.

Some forty or fifty young women in various costumes, from the imitation sealskin coat and hat with a dyed feather in it, to the rusty black merino of some poor widow, are to be seen chatting and waiting in hope of being chosen to represent Peris of Paradise or Inhabitants of the Moon as the transformation scene may require.

Some few are eligible at a glance – smart, well-formed, tidy-looking girls; some are equally certain not to be 'cast' – draggled, disreputable and impossible. There is no doubt about these; but the unpleasant part of selecting is the elimination of some respectable women who are hoping, in spite of all, to add a weekly pittance to their homes, and yet possess nothing – neither height, charm, nor any personal qualifications – fitting them to appear as a decorative item in the Houris' Home of Eternal Happiness, where the houris, too slightly clad, are passing a very unpleasant quarter of an hour, strapped to irons, and inhaling the fumes of magnesium and red fire.

However, it has to be done; and, after all, those not chosen will go to some minor theatre where the houris are happier and the gods not so difficult to please. Our thirty extras have been selected, and will appear on Boxing Night in all the glories of gold tissue, enhanced by the limelight's rays . . .

Nothing, perhaps, is more tedious than a scene-rehearsal. You sit with the scenic artists in the stalls or the circles – sometimes in one, sometimes in the other – to judge of the artistic effect, and to dispose the lighting of the various sets or pictures. The fly-men (that is, the carpenters up aloft), the cellar-men (those below the stage), and the stage-carpenters have never yet worked together; and it appears almost marvellous, looking at the crowded cloths and borders, wings and ground-pieces, with the complicated ropes and pulleys above, and cuts and bridges in the stage, not to mention the traps and sliders, gas-battens and ladders, how a series of fifteen and sixteen scenes, besides the elaborate transformation scene, which, perhaps, demands the united skill of fifty or sixty men to work its marvels and develop its mysterious beauties, can even be worked with such systematic regularity and unerring correctness. A good master-carpenter is a general, and all his men depend on his head in time of action. Then there are the gas-men, who have to raise or subdue the floats or footlights, the ground-rows, the wing-ladders, the battens or border-lights, and the bunch-lights or portable suns, which are required to give one effect to a brilliant tropical landscape or a bewilderingly luxurious palace. The limelights also have their special guardians. Each head of a department makes his special list of effects and changes, and notes the alterations or indications made at rehearsals; in fact, a large theatre at Christmas time, or whenever a spectacle of unusual splendour is to be produced, is a little world in itself, and no ant-hills, no bee-hive can be busier or more occupied . . .

To judge really of the hive a theatre becomes during pantomime season, go to Covent Garden or Drury Lane, and when you watch the masses of actors, actresses, and figurants on the stage, think of the labourers you do not see, and the mouths that annually depend on these shows to make both ends meet before the spring comes again.

It Came Upon the Midnight Clear

Edmund Sears

In the mid-nineteenth century antiquarians and musicologists were in the process of collecting or rediscovering carols, many of which were in danger of being forgotten through general lack of interest. Clergymen were encouraged to make carols in church a part of Christmas worship, and several new carol books were published. Sullivan was fortunate to be growing up at a time when new carols were being written to cater for the demand, and when composers were setting traditional festive verses to music. The words to this ever-popular song were originally written and published by Edmund Sears in 1849, the original music being composed by Richard Willis; an alternative melody was composed by Sullivan as one of his Five Sacred Part-Songs, 1871.

It came upon the midnight clear,
That glorious song of old
From angels bending near the earth
To touch their harps of gold:
'Peace on the earth, goodwill to men,
From heav'n's all-gracious King.'
The world in solemn stillness lay
To hear the angels sing.
Still through the cloven skies they come,
With peaceful wings unfurled,
And still their heavenly music floats
O'er all the weary world.
Above its sad and lowly plains,

They bend on hovering wing;
And ever o'er its Babel sound
The blessed angels sing.

And ye, beneath life's crushing load,
Whose forms are bending low,
Who toil along the climbing way
With painful steps and slow,
Look now! for glad and golden hours
Come swiftly on the wing.
O rest beside the weary road,
And hear the angels sing.
For lo, the days are hastening on,
By prophet seen of old,
When, with the ever-circling years,
Shall come the time foretold,

'It came upon the midnight clear'. Sullivan wrote the opening bars of his setting to the hymn to be published with an interview by Arthur Lawrence, published in *The Strand Magazine*, December 1897

When the new heaven and earth shall own
The Prince of Peace their King,
And the whole world send back the song
Which now the angels sing.

Burnand's Dickensian Christmas

Sir F.C. Burnand

Francis Cowley Burnand (1836–1917), born in the same year as
Gilbert, was also called to the bar as a young man, but forsook a
legal career for journalism and drama, becoming one of the original
founders of Fun *before going to work for* Punch, *which he edited*
from 1880 to 1906. He was knighted in 1902. Had Gilbert never
been introduced to the composer, the most famous Savoy operas
might have been written by Burnand and Sullivan, as they had
collaborated on the one-act Cox and Box *and the less successful* The
Contrabandista, *revised seventeen years later (after Gilbert & Sullivan*
had suspended their partnership following the 'carpet quarrel') as The
Chieftain. *Though he continued to enjoy success as a dramatist,*
Burnand was probably jealous of the man who had become Sullivan's
most famous librettist. His farce of 1880, The Colonel, *a satire on the*
aesthetic movement, pre-dated Patience *by some months. He was so*
annoyed by the latter, which in his view amounted to plagiarism, that
he refused to allow a review of it to appear in Punch.
In Records and Reminiscences, *published in 1903, he recalled*
his childhood 'Dickensian Christmas'. Arthur and Toney were
his uncle and aunt.

Arthur Burnand and Toney were devoted to music, opera and theatricals. They always had one or two young ladies staying in the house, to one of whom my uncle was invariably supposed to be attached; but the ladies were changed from time to time, and my uncle remained a bachelor, as my aunt remained a spinster, until first one, then the other died, at about seventy years of age. They were devoted to children, and their married brothers and sisters had been thoughtful enough to provide a considerable number of additions to the Burnand family, on whom the bachelor uncle and maiden aunt could expend as much time and money, especially at Christmas time, as might seem good to them.

What Christmases these were! At first, of course, my recollection of them is now somewhat dim, but gradually as I arrived at the mature years of seven, eight, and upwards, I can look back on these Christmas festivals as occasions ever memorable, serving me, many, many years afterwards, when my wife and I being the entertainers, our children were as I was when I used to be taken to my grandfather's house, as models, so to speak, for our home festivals and family gatherings, revivified and renewed, after an interval of 'many changing years.' Such festivals have been among the happiest times of our lives, even though our happiness has gradually come to be tempered by some sadness. 'How many old recollections, and how many dormant sympathies does Christmas time awaken!' exclaims Charles Dickens in his delightful and ever-fresh chapter concerning the seasonable festivities at Dingley

Dell. And he continues: 'We write these words now, many miles distant from the spot at which, year after year, we met on that day, a merry and joyous circle. Many of the hearts that throbbed so gaily then have ceased to beat; many of the looks that shone so brightly then have ceased to glow; the hands we grasped have grown cold; the eyes we sought have hid their lustre in the grave; and yet the old house, the room, the merry voices and smiling faces, the jest, the laugh, the most minute and trivial circumstances connected with those happy meetings, crowd on our mind at each recurrence of the season, as if the last assemblage had been but yesterday! Happy, happy Christmas, that can win us back to the delusions of our childish days; that can recall to the old man the pleasure of his youth, that can transport the sailor and the traveller thousands of miles away, back to his own fireside and his quiet home!'

The modern school of writers shrug their shoulders over this, and pronounce it 'bathos or clap-trap.' Personally I believe Dickens felt intensely every word of it; and, personally, I can read this passage over and over again, Christmas after Christmas, and exclaim, with the orator who couldn't make a speech, without descending into bathos or becoming sentimental, 'My own sentiments, sir, only infinitely better expressed.'

However, this is not a disquisition on Christmas, not an excursion into the small state of which Charles Lamb was 'every inch a king'; so being only 'reminiscences,' as Mr. Sam Weller might have explained, 'my vision and remarks are limited.'

Upon The Snow-Clad Earth

Traditional

Sullivan set music to this carol in an arrangement published in 1876.

Upon the snow-clad earth without,
The stars are shining bright,
As Heaven had hung out all her lamps
To hail our festal night;
For on this night, long years ago,
The Blessed babe was born,
The saints of old were wont
To keep their vigils until morn.

'Twas in the days when far and wide
Men owned the Caesar's sway,
That his decree went forth, that all
A certain tax should pay.
Then from their home in Nazareth's vale,
Obedient to the same,
With Mary, his espoused wife,
The saintly Joseph came.

A stable and a manger, where
The oxen lowed around,
Was all the shelter Bethlehem gave,

The welcome that they found!
Yet blessed among women was
That holy mother-maid,
Who on that night her First-born son
There in the manger laid.

The KING of kings, and LORD of lords,
E'en from His very birth,
Had not a place to lay His Head,
An outcast in the earth;
And yet we know that little Babe
Was tender to the touch,

Cards like this caught the
popular sentiment.

And weak as other infants are,
He felt the cold as much.

In swaddling bands she wrapped Him round,
And smoothed His couch of straw.
While unseen Angels watched beside,
In mute, adoring awe.
How softly did they fold their wings
Beneath that star-lit shed,
While eastern Sages from afar
The new-born radiance led!

And thus it is, from age to age,
That as this night comes around,
So sweetly, underneath the moon,
The Christmas carols sound.
Because to us a CHILD is born,
Our BROTHER, and our KING,
Angels in Heaven, and we on earth,
Our joyful anthems sing.

Christmas at Eastwell Park

Marie, Queen of Roumania

One of Sullivan's greatest friends and admirers was Queen Victoria's second son Alfred, Duke of Edinburgh and later Duke of Saxe-Coburg Gotha (1844–1900), himself a keen violinist and occasional composer as well as patron of English music. In the first of three volumes of reminiscences, The Story of my Life *(1933–5), the duke's eldest daughter Marie, later Queen of Roumania (1875–1938), recalled Christmas and winter at their country seat, Eastwell Park, near Ashford, Kent. This extract vividly evokes the magic of the festive season through childhood eyes. Sullivan was a regular guest at Eastwell though he probably never spent Christmas there.*

One day, rare occurrence, there was a tremendous fall of snow and papa took us out for some tobogganing down a hill near the dairy. That was wonderful. I think it was the first snow I ever saw, and what child can resist the fascination of snow? But in England snow never lasts – it came and went like a scarcely realized dream.

But I also remember some skating on the big lake, and although we were but wee wobbly beginners, I can still feel the rapturous ecstasy of launching forth upon the shiny surface. The keen winter air made your eyes water and painted your cheeks and nose fiery red, but it was beyond words glorious. How I remember, too, the crumply round black velvet caps, trimmed with dark

Russian sable which we wore for this memorable occasion; these becoming little red caps still further enhanced the pleasure of skating as did also the sip of the hot cinnamon-flavoured red wine which was given us as the sun sank in the West.

Likewise of delightful memory was the apple- and pear-house, and I can still almost taste the aromatic flavour of the huge golden pear the gardener selected for me off one of the shelves where the fruit stood in tempting lines of green, red and yellow. Last but not least there was the excitement of Christmas!

The Christmas tree was set up in the big library, whilst the presents were laid out on white-covered tables all round the walls of the room. But what mysteries went on beforehand! Papa, especially, became tremendously important at this season; he liked occasionally to take things in hand, and became himself as eager as a child. But like all men he was excessively meticulous and could get very angry if the smallest detail he had planned was not religiously adhered to.

One of the fore-thrills of Christmas was the stirring of the servants' plum pudding. This ceremony took place in the steward's room, and also in the official part of the stables, because house and stables were two separate realms and one never dared overlap the other. The etiquette amongst the servants of a well-organized English household is all-important. An enormous bowl was set upon the table and each child had to have a 'go' at the stirring, which was a stiff job, but of immense consequence.

Princesses Marie and Victoria Melita of Edinburgh

At last Christmas Eve was there, and the library doors, which had been kept closed for several days, were thrown open, and there stood the tree, a blaze of light, and all around upon the white-decked tables, one mass of gifts for everybody, no one ever being forgotten.

Oh, glorious moment of realization! And, rather shyly, holding each other's hands, we children advanced towards all that light, till we stood in the very centre of it, were part of it ourselves.

For many, many a year the thrill of Christmas held good, the days of secret preparation beforehand, the hushed silence before the closed door and then the sudden fulfilment in a blaze of candlelight, accompanied by the delicious fragrance of singed fir-branches so inseparable from Christmas. Later the trouble and care of sorting, preparing, organizing became our share; the thrill, the ecstasy of fulfilment had passed over to the younger generation, but all through my life in the far land of my adoption I tried to make the Christmases I arranged as much as possible like the Eastwell, and later the Malta Christmases. [*The family spent a few years at Malta during Marie's adolescence, when her father was commander-in-chief of the Mediterranean fleet*]. For those will ever be the Christmases that remain most unforgettable to me.

Hints on Christmas Shopping

Punch may have seen fit to reject some of Gilbert's more savage ballads, although its pages were open to the equally cruel humour of others, as this piece of rather anarchic advice 'By a good Old-fashioned Clown' (6 January 1872) demonstrates.

Knock at a shop-door, and then lie down flat in front of it, so that the shopman, coming out, may tumble head-long over you. Then bolt into the shop, and cram into your pockets all the big things you can find, so that in trying to get out, you cannot squeeze them through the doorway. For instance, if it be a watchmaker's, clasp an eight-day kitchen clock and a barometer or two, let us say, in your right pocket, and a brass warming-pan, or some such little article of jewellery (as you will take care to call it) in your left one; taking pains, of course, to let the handle stick well out if it. If it be a butcher's, pouch a leg of beef and half a sheep or so, and be sure not to forget to bring a yard or two of sausages trailing on the ground behind you. Then if you can't squeeze through the doorway, the simplest plan will be to jump clean through the shop-front, and in doing this take care to smash as any panes of glass as you are able, crying out, of course, that you took 'great pains' to do so. *En passant*, you will kick into the street whatever goods are in the window, and then run off as quickly as your heels can carry you.

If the shopman should pursue you, as most probably he

'We children advanced towards that light' A recreation of a typical Victorian Christmas table setting. (Christmas Archives)

will, make him a low bow, and say that it was really quite an accident, and that of course you mean to pay him – indeed, yes, 'on your *honour!*' If he won't believe you, punch him in the waistcoat, and batter him about with his barometer and warming-pan, or sausages and mutton.

Should a policeman interfere, and want to know what you are up to, catch up your red-hot poker (which you will always have about you), and hold it hidden behind your back, while you beg him to shake hands with you, because you mean to 'squeeze the job' with him. Then, when he puts his hand out, slap the poker into it, and run away as fast as your stolen goods will let you.

But after a few steps, of course you must take care to let the handle of your warming-pan get stuck between your legs, and trip you up occasionally; and you will manage that your sausages become entangled so about you that, at every second step, you are obliged to tumble down and roll along the ground, and double up into a heap, till the policeman, who keeps up the chace, comes close enough to catch you. Then you will spring up again, and jumping on his back, you will be carried off to Bow Street, with the small boys shouting after you; or, else, if you prefer it, you may 'bonnet' the policeman, and run away and hide yourself ere he can lift his hat up to see where you are gone to.

A Really New Christmas Number

Though Gilbert had long ceased contributing to Punch *by 1877, the year in which their first full-length opera to survive in its entirety,* The Sorcerer, *was playing, his sense of irony would surely have relished this piece from the Christmas issue (22 December).*

At this time of the year the shops are deluged with Christmas numbers, in which Yule-tide is painted in the most glowing colours. Snow, robins, and good cheer abound in these so-called seasonable Annuals. For a novelty, Mr. Punch suggests that a grand extra number shall be published, by all the periodical-publishers in concert, in which Christmas shall be depicted as it is. Were this done, the following circular might be issued immediately:-

'Compliments of the Season'. *Punch*, 6 January 1872. The gentleman commiserates with the yokel on his newly-acquired black-eye, to be told he gets the same present every year . . .

'Here we are again!'. *Punch*, 25 December 1880. Mr. Punch is the bibulous old gentleman on the right.

DREARY CHRISTMAS!

Mr. Punch begs to announce the United Publishers' grand Yule-tide Annual.

Amongst the Illustrations will be found 'A Row in a Family Party;' 'The Doctor's Visit to the Nursery on Boxing-Day;' 'The Man in Possession on Christmas-Eve;' 'The Christmas Sermon – TOMMIE fast Asleep;' 'Christmas in Seven Dials – Thrashing the Missus;' 'Putting up Umbrellas on Christmas-Day,' &c., &c.

The following seasonable Stories have been written for Dreary Christmas: – 'How JOHNNY NOGO spent Christmas-Day in the Debtors' Ward of Holloway Prison;' 'The Story of the Clown who Used a real red-hot Poker;' 'How ARCHIE MUDDLECASH found a Writ in a Christmas Pudding;' 'How a Certain Christmas was spent in Lodgings at Herne Bay,' 'Christmas-Day at Doctor Birch's Boarding-School, and how the Anglo-Indian Scholars enjoyed it;' 'Why DAN PERRIWINKLE tried to Hang Himself on Boxing-Day,' &c., &c.

Besides the above, Dreary Christmas will be adorned with a magnificent double-page Illustration, entitled, 'Bringing in the Christmas Bills,' printed in black and white, with an emblematical border of funereal arabesques founded on the famous Danse-Macabre of the Fourteenth Century, in which, instead of Death arresting all conditions of men, Father Christmas will be represented leaving his bills on representatives of all classes and callings.

My Pantomime

W.S. Gilbert

Long after Gilbert had ceased to concentrate on writing pantomime, he continued to reminiscence on the theme. This article (which for once he did not illustrate with his drawings) appeared in the Era Almanack, *1884.*

I once wrote a Pantomime. It didn't succeed. It was not my fault. This is the history of a good many plays, written by a good many authors. It is seldom the author's fault when a play don't succeed. I know this to be a fact because I have heard them say so. I am sure it was a fact with regard to my pantomime. I wrote it many years ago – seventeen years ago, I think – for the late Mr. E.T. Smith, who was the lessee of the Lyceum Theatre. I got sixty pounds for it – eventually. It was called 'Harlequin Cock Robin and Jenny Wren, and the Little Man who had a Little Gun.' I don't think it was a good title, but Mr. E.T. Smith thought it was. Perhaps it was as good as any other. There was a procession of birds in it, and every bird was, somehow, exactly like the lessee.

The piece was written in four days and produced in about three weeks after it was commenced. For some reason which I forget, the preliminary rehearsals had to take place in the 'saloon' of the theatre – but we got on to the stage after the first ten days or so. It was intended that the rather accentuated 'Finette' troup should be a prominent feature of this pantomime, and the distinguished foreigners were received with a round of applause when they presented themselves on the stage during a night rehearsal, after a very stormy passage across the Channel, during which they had all been horribly ill. They looked white – dirty white – but their pluck was indomitable. The stage manager asked if they were prepared to rehearse their quadrille. They replied that they were not, but they would be in half a minute. Hats, cloaks, wraps were cast off – and eventually, I am bound to add, their dresses also – and in their petticoat bodies they went through their business with extraordinary spirit. The company was highly scandalized – but the costume might have been worse. For instance, it might have been the costume in which they eventually played.

Mr. E.T. Smith had bought a vast crystal fountain, and this property was to be the principal scenic effect of the pantomime. Four scenes had to be introduced to give time to 'set' this absurdity and three scenes to strike it. Most of these scenes were written by the stage manager, who, when I expostulated, told me they were much better written than mine, and Mr. Smith agreed with him. Perhaps they were right. I remember that the scenes contained several allusions to 'Powder Blue,' and some kind of starch which was then popular. When the piece came to be played, I discovered (I was dramatically young at the time) that a reference to 'Powder Blue' always brought down the house. It didn't matter how,

The Mikado, 1979, Christmas card by Geoffrey Shovelton (by kind permission of the artist)

why, or when it was introduced –
it was a safe roar. In fact, all the
laughs in the piece were the stage
manager's. I was rude to him at
the time, but I apologise to him
now. The rehearsals were, of
course, a wild scramble. Every-

body was going to introduce a song or a dance
(unknown to me), and these songs and dances were
rehearsed surreptitiously in corners. One gentleman who
played a king with a false skull piece covered with red
spots (he was dressed for his part), was open and candid
with me, but he was sly as against everybody else. He
took me aside and he began by binding me to implicit
secrecy as to what he was about to communicate. He
then told me that he wished to show me a dance which
he intended to introduce. I agreed to look at it and
begged him to proceed. 'Not here, Sir,' said he. 'Bless
your eyes, if So-and-So (another monarch with moveable
hair) were to see it, he'd snap it up in a minute. Follow
me!' He procured a large lantern, lighted it, we
descended into the bowels of the earth below the stage.
Eventually he stopped in a little dark damp cellar at the
back of everything. He then placed the lantern on the
ground and solemnly began to dance at me. The lantern
lighted his legs and nothing else, and the terrific spectacle
of those weird and wizened limbs dancing a collar-flap
by themselves haunted my dreams for many a night after.
I wish I could have seen myself looking at those phantom

legs. They were striped red and white like a stick of peppermint. Shuddering with horror I approved the dance, and he took up the lantern and became a kind of human being once more. Enough – I don't like to think of it.

The piece was produced on Boxing-night. It was an amazing production. It had occurred to Mr. E.T. Smith that it would be a good idea to have the scenery painted at Cremorne (of which he was lessee), and carted up to the Lyceum. The scenery was all behind – at least, it was none of it behind – it was all at Cremorne. At about four o'clock on Boxing-day instalments of the scenery began to arrive – three pairs of wings, then half a flat, then a couple of sky borders, and so on. When the curtain rose on the piece about three complete scenes had arrived. Two of these were scenes that had been introduced to set the fountain. They were to have occurred late in the opening, but they were served up hot and cold as they arrived. Then came a ballet scene – all perfect except the cloth. Then an apology by Mr. E.T. Smith. Then came two more scenes introduced to set the fountain, and the three scenes introduced to strike it. (The fountain never appeared in the pantomime at all; but the scenes introduced to set it and strike it were retained on account of their valuable allusions to Powder Blue). The last of these three scenes was a forest scene. It was to be followed by the transformation scene; but the transformation scene was not ready. So a very clever lady, who rendered invaluable services on this eventful evening, went on and sang 'Not for Joe.' Then came a pause. Then an excited dialogue was heard at the wing:–

Mr. Smith. Go on, somebody! And do something! Here – *you* go on!
Voice. Please, Sir, I'm for the comic scenes.
Mr. Smith. Bless the comic scenes! Cross the stage at once!

And immediately a plum pudding on two legs hopped to the centre of the stage, turned to the audience, bowed politely, turned towards the opposite wing, and hopped off.

Mr. Smith. Now you!
Voice. Me, Sir, please, Sir?
Mr. Smith. Yes, Sir, you. Cross the stage!

Enter a small Policeman. Bows to audience. Exit small Policeman.

Mr. Smith. Now the ballet. Quick! The Fish Ballet.
Voice (in expostulation – probably Ballet Master). A fish ballet in a forest?
Mr. Smith (maddened). *Is* this a time to talk of forests?

The Ballet Master probably agreed with Mr. Smith (on reflection) that this was *not* a time to talk of forests, for a 'Fish Ballet' entered (very shiny and scaly, but otherwise not like any fish I have ever met), and danced a long ballet, which they themselves thoughtfully encored. Then

came the clever and hardworking lady with another song (from last year's pantomime). Then a can-can by the Finette troupe. Then a party of acrobats. Then the spotted monarch's mystic dance. Altogether a chain of events calculated to arrest the attention of a wayfarer through that wood and set him pondering. At last came the transformation scene – that is to say, some of it. One half of the scene – the O.P. half – was there; tinselled fenelly branches, with large, half-opened oyster shells beneath each branch, each shell containing a beautiful young lady. It is not considered a healthy sign when oyster shells open by themselves; but in this case the contents looked quite fresh. But the other half of the scene – the P.S. half – alas! – it hadn't arrived – it was at Cremorne! There was no attempt to fill up the deficiency. One half of the stage was complete, the other half was empty. Mr. Smith (he was a bold man) rushed on to the stage amid a storm of execrations. The noise was awful. I don't know what he said; *he* didn't know what he said. He told me afterwards that he merely opened his mouth as if he were speaking, but that he said nothing. At last he concluded with a pleasant smile and a polite bow, and backed off. Suddenly the humour of the house changed, and a round of applause greeted his exit. He had not uttered an audible word, but he had convinced the house nevertheless. The comic scenes went excellently. The clever lady who sang the songs sang some more. The pantomimists, who had had to rehearse their scenes in the greenroom, did their extemporised best, and were received with much favour. The pantomime did not succeed eventually, notwithstanding the briskness of the scenes introduced to set and strike the fountain, which never came; but Mr. Smith's inaudible speech at least saved the pantomime from utter condemnation on the first night.

All This Night Bright Angels Sing

William Austin

The words to this carol were written by William Austin in about 1630, and Sullivan's music to them was published in 1902, two years after his death.

> All this night bright angels sing,
> Never was such carolling:
> Hark! A voice which loudly cries,
> 'Mortals, mortals, wake and rise.
> Lo! To gladness
> Turns your sadness;
> From the earth is ris'n a Son,
> Shines all night, though day be done.'

'Carol for Christmas Day' – All this night bright angels sing. (Music by Sir Arthur Sullivan)

Wake, O earth, wake everything,
Wake and hear the joy I bring:
Wake and joy; for all this night,
Heaven and every twinkling light,
All amazing,
Still stand gazing;
Angels, Powers, and all that be,
Wake, and joy this Sun to see!

Hail! O Sun, O blessed Light,
Sent into this world by night:
Let Thy rays and heav'nly pow'rs
Shine in these dark souls of ours.
For, most duly,
Thou art truly;
God and man, we do confess;
Hail, O Sun of Righteousness!

Christmas on the Ocean Wave

Henry Lytton and Martyn Green

*Following the death of Richard D'Oyly Carte in April 1901, four and
a half months after that of Sullivan, his widow Helen took over
direction of the opera company bearing his name, and on her death in
1913 her place was taken by her stepson Rupert. When the company's
annual London season ended on 18 December 1926 they sailed from
Liverpool for Canada, where they gave their first performance on
4 January 1927. Henry Lytton (1865–1936), principal comedian,
and Martyn Green (1899–1975), playing smaller parts, were
among the members, and both recalled the journey and festivities in
their memoirs, Lytton's account being from* A Wandering
Minstrel *(1933).*

My first visit there [Canada] was seven years ago, in 1926,
and I shall never forget setting out from England to make
the journey. It was Christmas Eve when we left Liverpool,
and there was sadness mixed with the excitement of going
to a new country. Anyone who has sailed out from
Liverpool knows that the last thing one sees of England is
the top of the huge Liver buildings. When they have gone
out of sight, having melted in the mists, England too seems
to have gone temporarily. On this Christmas Eve, I
remember, all the decks were crowded with people, many
of whom did not expect to be coming back. All of them
were watching and waiting, craning to see through the

ever-thickening mists the one last glimpse of the great Liver buildings. Everybody always watches them.

At the quayside, before the ship set sail, there had been laughter and cheers, the waving of handkerchiefs to relatives and friends who were being left behind. But long after the friends could be seen no more the lights of Liverpool flickered; then gradually they melted into the mists, and the gigantic building stuck up like a huge rock with everyone on board waiting for the last sign of it to disappear.

But we soon developed into a happy ship. These farewells are always sad, but ship's officers, particularly at Christmas-time, know how to overcome the sadness and replace it with joy in the hearts of everybody. We were on the good ship *Metagama*, and with me were sixty members of the Gilbert and Sullivan Company. On Christmas morning, when we woke up on board, we found that the ship had been cheerfully decorated with flags and the stewards seemed to be buzzing and running about hither and thither all over the deck, bringing wireless messages – Christmas greetings to, it seemed, everybody on board from their friends ashore. Throughout the day we seemed to be in constant communication with the homeland, and it was a very comforting feeling.

The day was not very old before real Yuletide fun commenced. While the last of the arrangements were being made for the day's entertainment, I remember, we were kept in constant laughter by a dear old gentleman who had crossed the Atlantic many times and had a rich and seemingly endless supply of sea stories. Each time he told one – or so it seemed to me – someone bought him a drink, and he was treated to round after round until I began to wonder how it was possible for anyone to drink so much without becoming unconscious. I was so surprised that I asked a steward.

'Ah, sir, he's all right,' replied the steward. 'He can drink any amount. He's got hollow legs.' Which caused another good laugh to go round the company.

Henry Lytton as the Duke of Plaza-Toro in *The Gondoliers*

I, ready to contribute what little I could to the general gaiety on such an occasion, accepted a suggestion that I should act as Father Christmas. But I was a queer Father Christmas, I am afraid, for instead of wearing a red cloak and hood and a flowing white beard I was dressed up as a chef and put into a huge pie. The pie was put on a trolley, and the scheme was to wheel it into the middle of the assembled ship's company, cut a slice off the pie to allow me to emerge, and then for me to distribute a gift to everyone on the ship. The idea went very well so far as the company was concerned, but not too well for me at the beginning because of a practical joke of which I was the victim.

'Come on, Lytton, you will have to hurry,' a group of me said to me. 'They are all ready to wheel you in. Come on, jump into the pie.'

I was squeezed into the pie, and had to sit there with my legs crossed and with a huge lid on top of me for over half an hour. I discovered afterwards that they were not ready for me, but everybody thought it was a hugely funny joke that I should have been shut up for such a long time that when I did emerge, instead of looking the personification of happiness, I was flustered and red, could hardly breathe, and felt ready to burst. But it gave everybody a good laugh, in which I joined as soon as I could fill my lungs with air, and we had a very jolly time.

In the evening the Gilbert and Sullivan Company gave a very fine concert. With sixty members of the company on board it was not difficult to draw up a very good programme, which delighted everybody and resulted in quite a nice sum being collected for charity.

Martyn Green, who became principal comedian and thus inherited the roles played by Lytton on the latter's retirement in 1933, remembered a couple of different incidents in Here's a How-de-do: Travelling with Gilbert and Sullivan *(1952).*

Apart from the natural excitement of a London Season there was, that year, a subdued excitement due to the fact that just one week after the season closed in the middle of December the Company was to embark for Canada on its first coast-to-coast tour. The last performance at the Prince's *[Theatre, London]* was on 18 December, and we were to sail from Liverpool on Christmas Eve.

It was the first ocean trip for the majority of us, and we intended to make the most of it. Christmas Day found us somewhere off the coast of Northern Ireland in glorious calm warm weather. Of about eighty Cabin passengers fifty were members of the D'Oyly Carte Opera Company. There was a number of children on board and presents for them hanging from a huge Christmas Tree in the main lounge. To everyone's dismay it turned out that their numbers had been miscalculated and that some of them had no presents. Everyone thought this was hard lines and decided there was nothing they could do about it; but Doris Hemingway (now Mrs. Harry Norris) found a solution. We were sitting on deck between lunch and tea and further along

Charles Goulding was to be seen with closed eyes quietly z-z-z-ing away. Doris and I started to sing some carols. Quite quietly. After a while I had a wish to annoy Charles by singing them to him, but nothing would make him open even one eye. We then went away hoping to annoy somebody else, and various couples in the drawing room threw money at us to make us go away. At this Doris had her great idea. We remembered the children and their Christmas presents, and for the next three quarters of an hour we toured the ship, picking up recruits as we went. We went to the Engine Room and sang to the Engineers; to the Galley, where we sang Carols to the Chef; to the officers' quarters, where we sang to the Officers on Watch. We explained our mission and collected money as we went, and we finished up in the Purser's Office, handing over to him enough to buy all the kids a couple of presents and still leave some over for the Seamen's Charities.

Christmas Day at Kirkby Cottage

Anthony Trollope

Anthony Trollope (1815–82) was the most prolific and widely read of English novelists in Gilbert & Sullivan's heyday, after the death of Charles Dickens in 1870. He was one of several notables mentioned in Colonel Calverley's song in Act I of Patience:

> The dash of a D'Orsay, divested of quackery –
> Narrative powers of Dickens and Thackeray –
> Victor Emmanuel – peak-haunting Peveril –
> Thomas Aquinas, and Doctor Sacheverell –
> Tupper and Tennyson – Daniel Defoe –
> Anthony Trollope and Mr Guizot! Ah!

On 17 May, six weeks after Patience *opened, Trollope and Sullivan were among guests at a dinner party given by the painter John Everett Millais, and in his diary the composer noted that he won £6 off the author, presumably at cards.*

Trollope, like Gilbert in his early days, wrote several Christmas stories for the Victorian magazine market, though he candidly admitted to disliking such tales that were meant to decorate magazines and journals 'like Christmas ornaments', and could not write stories like Dickens, full of spirits, ghosts of Christmas past and impossibly angelic small children. He preferred to 'avoid the humbug and have an honest story to tell', setting his stories at Christmas time but concentrating on plots arising from the characters themselves 'and their awareness that the season imposes a special demand on them to be charitable beyond the usual and at peace with those around them'.

In this extract from a tale first published in Routledge's Christmas

Annual, *1870, he describes the festive season at the Yorkshire rectory
of the Rev. John Lownd, his daughters Isabel (20) and Mabel (14),
and their guest Maurice Archer.*

'After all, Christmas is a bore!'

'Even though you should think so, Mr. Archer, pray do
not say so here.'

'But it is.'

'I am very sorry that you should feel like that; but pray
do not say anything so very horrible.'

'Why not? And why is it horrible? You know very well
what I mean.'

'I do not want to know what you mean; and it would
make papa very unhappy if he were to hear you.'

'A great deal of beef is roasted, and a great deal of
pudding is boiled, and the people try to be jolly by eating
more than usual. The consequence is, they get very
sleepy, and want to go to bed an hour before the proper
time. That's Christmas.'

He who made this speech was a young man about
twenty-three years old, and the other personage in the
dialogue was a young lady, who might be, perhaps, three
years his junior. The 'papa' to whom the lady had
alluded was the Rev. John Lownd, parson of Kirkby
Cliffe, in Craven, and the scene was the parsonage
library, as pleasant a little room as you would wish to
see, in which the young man who thought Christmas to
be a bore was at present sitting over the fire, in the
parson's arm chair, with a novel in his hand, which he

had been reading till he was interrupted by the parson's daughter. It was nearly time for him to dress for dinner, and the young lady was already dressed. She had entered the room on the pretext of looking for some book or paper, but perhaps her main object may have been to ask for some assistance from Maurice Archer in the work of decorating the parish church. The necessary ivy and holly branches had been collected, and the work was to be performed on the morrow. The day following would be Christmas Day. It must be acknowledged, that Mr. Archer had not accepted the proposition made to him very graciously.

Maurice Archer was a young man as to whose future career in life many of his elder friends shook their heads and expressed much fear. It was not that his conduct was dangerously bad, or that he spent his money too fast, but that he was abominably conceited, so said these elder friends; and then there was the unfortunate fact of his being altogether beyond control. He had neither father, nor mother, nor uncle, nor guardian. He was the owner of a small property not far from Kirkby Cliffe, which gave him an income of some six or seven hundred a year, and he had altogether declined any of the professions which had been suggested to him. He had, in the course of the year now coming to a close, taken his degree at Oxford, with some academical honours, which were not high enough to confer distinction, and had already positively refused to be ordained, although, would he do so, a small living would be at his disposal on the death of a septuagenarian cousin. He intended, he said, to farm a portion of his own land, and had already begun to make amicable arrangements for buying up the interest of one of his two tenants. The rector of Kirkby Cliffe, the Rev. John Lownd, had been among his father's dearest friends, and he was now the parson's guest for the Christmas . . .

It had been chiefly at Mabel's instigation that Isabel had invited the co-operation of her father's visitor in the adornment of the church for Christmas day. Isabel had expressed her opinion that Mr. Archer didn't care a bit about such things, but Mabel declared that she had already extracted a promise from him. 'He'll do anything I ask him,' said Mabel, proudly. Isabel, however, had not cared to undertake the work in such company, simply under her sister's management, and had proffered the request herself. Maurice had not declined the task, – had indeed promised his assistance in some indifferent fashion,

A Victorian phantasy – sleigh ride across the snow.

– but had accompanied his promise by a suggestion that Christmas was a bore! Isabel had rebuked him, and then he had explained. But his explanation, in Isabel's view of the case, only made the matter worse. Christmas was to her a very great affair indeed, – a festival to which the roast beef and the plum pudding were, no doubt, very necessary; but not by any means the essence, as he had chosen to consider them. Christmas a bore! No; a man who thought Christmas to be a bore should never be more to her than a mere acquaintance. She listened to his explanation, and then left the room, almost indignantly. Maurice, when she was gone, looked after her, and then read a page of his novel; but he was thinking of Isabel, and not of the book. It was quite true that he had never said a word to her that might not have been declared from the church tower; but, nevertheless, he had thought about her a good deal. Those were days on which he was sure that he was in love with her, and would make her his wife. Then there came days on which he ridiculed himself for the idea. And now and then there was a day on which he asked himself whether he was sure that she would take him were he to ask her. There was sometimes an air with her, some little trick of the body, a manner of carrying her head when in his presence, which he was not physiognomist enough to investigate, but which in some way suggested doubts to him. It was on such occasions as this that he was most in love with her; and now she had left the room with that particular motion of her head which seemed almost to betoken contempt.

'If you mean to do anything before dinner you'd better do it at once,' said the parson, opening the door. Maurice jumped up, and in ten minutes was dressed and down in the dining-room. Isabel was there, but did not greet him. 'You'll come and help us to-morrow,' said Mabel, taking him by the arm and whispering to him.

'Of course I will,' said Maurice.

'And you won't go to Hundlewick again till after Christmas?'

'It won't take up the whole day to put up the holly.'

'Yes it will, – to do it nicely, – and nobody ever does any work the day before Christmas.'

'Except the cook,' suggested Maurice.

Not a word was said about Christmas that evening. Isabel had threatened the young man with her father's displeasure on account of his expressed opinion as to the festival being a bore, but Mr. Lownd was not himself one who talked a great deal about any Church festival. Indeed, it may be doubted whether his more enthusiastic daughter did not in her heart think him almost too indifferent on the subject. In the decorations of the church he, being an elderly man and one with other duties to perform, would of course take no part. When the day came he would preach, no doubt, an appropriate sermon, would then eat his own roast beef and pudding with his ordinary appetite, would afterwards, if allowed to do so, sink into his arm-chair behind his book, – and then, for him, Christmas would be over. In all this there was no disrespect for the day, but it was hardly an enthusiastic observance. Isabel desired to greet the morning of her Saviour's birth with some special demonstration of joy. Perhaps from year to year she was somewhat disappointed, – but never before had it been hinted to her that Christmas was a bore.

We Sing a Song of Christmas-Time

A. Ernest Smith

A. Ernest Smith wrote this carol, to which Sullivan composed the music, probably at the end of the nineteenth century.

We sing a song of Christmas-time,
A day of glad festivity,
And, with voices ringing clear,
Hail the day of Christ's nativity.
From heaven He came with wondrous name,
A child to be;
On Christmas Day in manger lay,
For you and me.

Chorus
Ring out, glad bell, Noel! Noel!
The Christ is come

To make His home
And with us dwell:
Immanuel, Amen.

The shepherds heard, in wonder lost,
His name resounding through the sky;
And the thronging heaven'ly host,
Singing, Glory be to God on high!
From heaven He came, our love to claim,
Our King to be;
And sendeth still peace and goodwill,
To you and me.

We hear th'angelic song again,
And come with haste, like those of old,
Off'ring our Christmas gifts,
Bringing Him our love instead of gold.
From heaven He came, to suffer shame
On Calvary;
To lead the way to endless day,
For you and me.

A Stormbright Christmas Eve

A.C. Swinburne

*The death of Robert Browning at Venice on 12 December 1889
inspired Algernon Charles Swinburne (1837–1909) to write a
sequence of seven sonnets, all composed within three days of hearing
the news and published the following year. The third, below, refers
to Browning's own long poem of 1850,* Christmas Eve and
Christmas Day. *
Swinburne and Sullivan had collaborated on a song in 1874, 'Love
laid his sleepless head'; the poet was later lampooned in* Patience, *and
named in Robin Oakapple's song in Act I of* Ruddigore:

> *As a poet, I'm tender and quaint –*
> *I've passion and fervour and grace –*
> *From Ovid and Horace,*
> *To Swinburne and Morris,*
> *They all of them take a back place.*

A graceless doom it seems that bids us grieve:
Venice and winter, hand in deadly hand,
Have slain the lover of her sunbright strand
And singer of a stormbright Christmas Eve.
A graceless guerdon we that loved receive
For all our love, from that the dearest land
Love worshipped ever. Blithe and soft and bland,
Too fair for storm to scathe or fire to cleave,
Shone on our dreams and memories evermore

The domes, the towers, the mountains and the shore
That gird or guard thee, Venice: cold and black
Seems now the face we loved as he of yore.
We have given thee love – no stint, no stay, no lack:
What gift, what gift is this thou hast given us back?

The Earthly Paradise:
Apology

William Morris

William Morris (1834–96) may have been among those taking a back seat to Robin Oakapple, but this most energetic of nineteenth-century Renaissance men – artist, designer, poet and socialist – also wrote occasionally of Christmas. First published in 1868, this is an extract from a series of twenty-four narrative poems held together by a framework, a kind of Victorian Canterbury Tales.

Of Heaven or Hell I have no power to sing,
I cannot ease the burden of your fears,
Or make quick-coming death a little thing,
Or bring again the pleasure of past years,
Nor for my words shall ye forget your tears,
Or hope again for aught that I can say,
The idle singer of an empty day.
But rather, when aweary of your mirth,

From full hearts still unsatisfied ye sigh,
And, feeling kindly unto all the earth,
Grudge every minute as it passes by,
Made the more mindful that the sweet days die –
Remember me a little then I pray,
The idle singer of an empty day.

The heavy trouble, the bewildering care
That weighs us down who live and earn our bread,
These idle verses have no power to bear;
So let 'em sing of names rememberèd,
Because they, living not, can ne'er be dead,
Or long time take their memory quite away
From us poor singers of an empty day.

Dreamer of dreams, born out of my due time,
Why should I strive to set the crooked straight?
Let it suffice me that my murmuring rhyme
Beats with light wing against the ivory gate,
Telling a tale not too importunate
To those who in the sleepy region stay,
Lulled by the singer of an empty day.

Folk say, a wizard to a northern king
At Christmas-tide such wondrous things did show,
That through one window men beheld the spring,
And through another saw the summer glow,
And through a third the fruited vines a-row,
While still, unheard, but in its wonted way,
Piped the drear wind of that December day.

So with this Earthly Paradise it is,
If ye will read aright, and pardon me,
Who strive to build a shadowy isle of bliss
Midmost the beating of the steely sea,
Where tossed about all hearts of men must be;
Whose ravening monsters mighty men shall slay,
Not the poor singer of an empty day.

Mr Pooter's Christmas

George and Weedon Grossmith

Today George Grossmith (1847–1912) is remembered mainly as co-author, with his brother Weedon (1853–1919), of The Diary of a Nobody. *A masterpiece of whimsical humour, it was serialised in* Punch *in 1891–2 and published in book form in the latter year. Yet in his lifetime he was known not only as a journalist, including reporter of court proceedings for* The Times, *but also as an entertainer. He took leading comic baritone roles in several Gilbert & Sullivan productions, from* The Sorcerer *(as John Wellington Wells, the role originally written for Sullivan's brother Frederick, whose illness and death put paid to the idea), to* The Yeomen of the Guard. *Ever modest about his abilities on stage, when first offered a comic lead by Gilbert he suggested that perhaps a fine man with a fine voice was what was needed. Anxious to avoid hiring a prima donna, Gilbert assured Grossmith that that was just what he did not want.*

In these extracts from The Diary of a Nobody, *Chapters XII and XIII, narrator Mr Charles Pooter, his wife Carrie, son Lupin, and the Mutlar family (with whose daughter Lupin has an on-off engagement) experience the usual delights and tribulations of the season, including indigestion, over-exuberant guests, and unforeseen complications involving Christmas cards.*

DECEMBER 20. Went to Smirksons', the drapers, in the Strand, who this year have turned out everything in the shop and devoted the whole place to the sale of Christmas cards. Shop crowded with people, who seemed to take up the cards rather roughly, and, after a hurried glance at them, throw them down again. I remarked to one of the young persons serving, that carelessness appeared to be a disease with some purchasers. The observation was scarcely out of my mouth, when my thick coat-sleeve caught against a large pile of expensive cards in boxes one on top of the other, and threw them down. The manager came forward, looking very much annoyed, and picking up several cards from the ground, said to one of the assistants, with a palpable side-glance at me: 'Put these amongst the sixpenny goods; they can't be sold for a shilling now.' The result was, I felt it my duty to buy some of these damaged cards.

I had to buy more and pay more than intended. Unfortunately I did not examine them all, and when I got home I discovered a vulgar card with a picture of a fat nurse with two babies, one black and the other white, and the words: 'We wish Pa a Merry Christmas.' I tore up the card and threw it away. Carrie said the great disadvantage of going out in Society and increasing the number of our friends was, that we should have to send out nearly two dozen cards this year.

DECEMBER 21. To save the postman a miserable Christmas, we follow the example of all unselfish people, and send out our cards early. Most of the cards had fingermarks, which I did not notice at night. I shall buy all future cards in the daytime. Lupin (who, ever since he has had the appointment with a stock and share broker, does not seem overscrupulous in his dealings) told me never to rub out the pencilled price on the backs of the cards. I asked him why. Lupin said: 'Suppose your card is marked 9d. Well, all you have to do is pencil a 3 – and a long down-stroke after it – in front of the ninepence, and people will think you have given five times the price for it.'

DECEMBER 24. I am a poor man, but I would gladly give ten shillings to find out who sent me the insulting Christmas card I received this morning. I never insult people; why should they insult me? The worst part of the transaction is, that I find myself suspecting all my friends. The handwriting on the envelope is evidently disguised, being written sloping the wrong way. I cannot think either Gowing or Cummings would do such a mean thing. Lupin denied all knowledge of it, and I believe him; although I disapprove of his laughing and sympathizing with the offender. Mr Franching would be above such an act; and I don't think any of the Mutlars would descend to such a course. I wonder if Pitt, that impudent clerk at the office, did it? Or Mrs Birrell, the charwoman, or Burwin-Fosselton? The writing is too good for the former.

George Grossmith, from a contemporary postcard.

CHRISTMAS DAY. We caught the 10.20 train at Paddington, and spent a pleasant day at Carrie's mother's. The country was quite nice and pleasant, although the roads were sloppy. We dined in the middle of the day, just ten of us, and talked over old times. If everybody had a nice, uninterfering mother-in-law, such as I have, what a deal of happiness there would be in the world. Being all in good spirits, I proposed her health; and I made, I think, a very good speech.

I concluded, rather neatly, by saying: 'On an occasion like this – whether relatives, friends, or acquaintances – we are all inspired with good feelings towards each other. We are of one mind, and think only of love and friendship. Those who have quarrelled with absent friends should kiss and make up. Those who happily have not fallen out, can kiss all the same.'

I saw tears in the eyes of both Carrie and her mother, and must say I felt very flattered by the compliment. That dear old Reverend John Panzy Smith, who married us, made a most cheerful and amusing speech, and said he should act on my suggestion respecting the kissing. He then walked round the table and kissed all the ladies, including Carrie. Of course one did not object to this: but I was more than staggered when a young fellow named Moss, who was a stranger to me, and who had scarcely spoken a word through dinner, jumped up suddenly with a sprig of mistletoe, and exclaimed: 'Hulloh! I don't see why I shouldn't be in on this scene.' Before one could realise what he was about to do, he kissed Carrie and the rest of the ladies.

Fortunately the matter was treated as a joke, and we all laughed: but it was a dangerous experiment, and I felt very uneasy for a moment as to the result. I subsequently referred the matter to Carrie, but she said : 'Oh; he's not much more than a boy.' I said that he had a very large moustache for a boy. Carrie replied: 'I didn't say he was not a nice boy.'

DECEMBER 26. I did not sleep very well last night; I never do in a strange bed. I feel a little indigestion, which one must expect at this time of the year. Carrie and I returned to Town in the evening. Lupin came in late. He said he enjoyed his Christmas, and added: 'I feel as fit as a Lowther Arcade fiddle, and only require a little more "off" to feel as fit as a £500 Stradivarius.' I have long since given up trying to understand Lupin's slang, or asking him to explain it.

DECEMBER 27. I told Lupin I was expecting Gowing and Cummings to drop in tomorrow evening for a quiet game. I was in hope the boy would volunteer to stay in, and help to amuse them. Instead of which, he said: 'Oh, you had better put them off, as I have asked Daisy and Frank Mutlar to come.' I said I could not think of doing such a thing. Lupin said: 'Then I will send a wire, and put off Daisy.' I suggested that a post-card or letter would reach her quite soon enough, and would not be so extravagant.

Carrie, who had listened to the above conversation with apparent annoyance, directed a well-aimed shaft at Lupin. She said: 'Lupin, why do you object to Daisy meeting your father's friends? Is it because they are not good enough for her, or (which is equally possible) she is not good enough for them?' Lupin was dumbfounded, and could make no reply. When he left the room, I gave Carrie a kiss of approval.

DECEMBER 28. Lupin, on coming down to breakfast, said to his mother: 'I have not put off Daisy and Frank, and should like them to join Gowing and Cummings this evening.' I felt very pleased with the boy for this. Carrie said in reply: 'I am glad you let me know in time, as I can turn over the cold leg of mutton, dress it with a little parsley, and no one will know it has been cut.' She further said she would make a few custards, and stew some pippins, so that they would be cold by the evening.

Finding Lupin in good spirits, I asked him quietly if he really had any personal objection to either Gowing or Cummings. He replied: 'Not in the least. I think Cummings looks rather an ass, but that is partly due to his patronizing "the three-and-six-one-price hat company", and wearing a reach-me-down frockcoat. As for that perpetual brown velveteen jacket of Gowing's – why, he resembles an itinerant photographer.'

I said it was not the coat that made the gentleman, whereupon Lupin, with a laugh, replied: 'No, and it wasn't much of a gentleman who made their coats.'

We were rather jolly at supper, and Daisy made herself very agreeable, especially in the earlier part of the evening, when she sang. At supper, however, she said: 'Can you make tee-to-tums with bread?' and she commenced rolling pieces of bread, and twisting them round on the table. I felt this to be bad manners, but of course said nothing. Presently Daisy and Lupin, to my disgust, began throwing bread-pills at each other. Frank followed suit, and so did Cummings and Gowing, to my astonishment. They then commenced throwing hard pieces of crust, one piece catching me on the forehead, and making me blink. I said: 'Steady, please; steady!' Frank jumped up and said: 'Tum, tum; then the band played.'

I did not know what this meant, but they all roared, and continued the bread-battle. Gowing suddenly seized all the parsley off the cold mutton, and threw it full in my face. I looked daggers at Gowing, who replied: 'I say, it's no good trying to look indignant, with your hair full of parsley.' I rose from the table, and insisted that a stop should be put to this foolery at once. Frank Mutlar shouted: 'Time, gentlemen, please! Time!' and turned out the gas, leaving us in absolute darkness.

I was feeling my way out of the room, when I suddenly received a hard intentional punch at the back of my head. I said loudly: 'Who did that?' There was no answer; so I repeated the question, with the same result. I struck a match, and lighted the gas. They were all talking and laughing, so I kept my own counsel; but, after they had gone, I said to Carrie: 'The person who sent me that insulting post-card at Christmas was here to-night.'

DECEMBER 29. I had a most vivid dream last night. I woke up, and on falling asleep, dreamed the same dream over again precisely. I dreamt I heard Frank Mutlar telling his sister that he had not only sent me the insulting Christmas card, but admitted that he was the one who punched my head last night in the dark. As fate would have it, Lupin, at breakfast, was reading extracts from a letter he had just received from Frank.

I asked him to pass the envelope, that I might compare the writing. He did so, and I examined it by the side of the envelope containing the Christmas card. I detected a similarity in the writing, in spite of the attempted disguise. I passed them on to Carrie, who began to laugh. I asked her what she was laughing at, and she said the card was never addressed to me at all. It was 'L. Pooter', not 'C. Pooter'. Lupin asked to look at the direction and the card, and exclaimed with a laugh: 'Oh yes, Guv., it's meant for me.' I said: 'Are you in the habit of receiving insulting Christmas cards?' He replied: 'Oh yes, and of sending them too.'

In the evening Gowing called, and said he enjoyed himself very much last night. I took the opportunity to confide in him, as an old friend, about the vicious punch last night. He burst out laughing, and said: 'Oh, it was your head, was it? I know I accidentally hit something, but I thought it was a brick wall.' I told him I felt hurt, in both senses of the expression.

Princess Ida:
'I Built Upon a Rock'

W.S. Gilbert

One of the rare references among the operas of Gilbert & Sullivan to the winter season occurs in Act III of Princess Ida, *a song performed by the princess herself. Appropriately Sullivan composed the music to it 'in the bleak midwinter'. With only four days to go before the first performance, this was one of two songs not yet completed. After rehearsing the orchestra during the morning of New Year's Day 1884, Sullivan was unable to find a cab to take him home and wrote the melody in his head while trudging back in a severe snowstorm.*

I built upon a rock,
But ere Destruction's hand
Dealt equal lot
To Court and cot,
My rock had turned to sand!
I leant upon an oak,
But in the hour of need,

Alack-a-day,
My trusted stay
Was but a bruisèd reed!
Ah, faithless rock,
My simple faith to mock!
Ah, trait'rous oak,
Thy worthlessness to cloak.

I drew a sword of steel,
But when to home and hearth
The battle's breath
Bore fire and death,
My sword was just a lath!
I lit a beacon fire,
But on a stormy day
Of frost and rime,
In wintertime,
My fire had died away!
Ah, coward steel,
That fear can unanneal!
False fire in deed,
To fail me in my need!

In Memoriam

Alfred Tennyson

Princess Ida, *billed as 'A respectful Operatic Per-version of*
Tennyson's "The Princess"', was partly a reworking of Gilbert's The
Princess *(1870), itself a burlesque of Tennyson's 1847 poem of the*
same title. Alfred, Lord Tennyson (1809–92), the quintessential poet
of Queen Victoria's reign, was Poet Laureate from 1851 until his
death. He collaborated with Sullivan in an 'Ode for the Opening of
the Colonial and Indian Exhibition', performed at the Royal Albert
Hall in May 1886, and a play The Foresters, *which opened at*
Daly's Theatre, New York City, in March 1892. Two of the
131 poems comprising his In Memoriam *have a festive theme. They*
were written in memory of Arthur Henry Hallam, who was
engaged to the poet's sister Emily but died of a stroke at the age of
22 in 1833. The first, no. 30, was published in 1850; the second,
No. 78, in 1872.

With trembling fingers did we weave
The holly round the Christmas hearth;
A rainy cloud possess'd the earth,
And sadly fell our Christmas-eve.

At our old pastimes in the hall
We gambol'd, making vain pretence
Of gladness, with an awful sense
Of one mute Shadow watching all.

We paused: the winds were in the beech:
We heard them sweep the winter land;
And in a circle hand-in-hand
Sat silent, looking each at each.

Then echo-like our voices rang;
We sung, tho' every eye was dim,
A merry song we sang with him
Last year: impetuously we sang:

We ceased: a gentler feeling crept
Upon us: surely rest is meet:
'They rest,' we said, 'their sleep is sweet,'
And silence follow'd, and we wept.

Our voices took a higher range;
Once more we sang: 'They do not die
Nor lose their mortal sympathy,
Nor change to us, although they change;

'Rapt from the fickle and the frail
With gather'd power, yet the same,
Pierces the keen seraphic flame
From orb to orb, from veil to veil.'

Rise, happy morn, rise, holy morn,
Draw forth the cheerful day from night:
O Father, touch the east, and light
The light that shone when Hope was born.

* * *

Again at Christmas did we weave
The holly round the Christmas hearth;
The silent snow possess'd the earth,
And calmly fell our Christmas-eve:

The yule-log sparkled keen with frost,
No wing of wind the region swept,
But over all things brooding slept
The quiet sense of something lost.

As in the winters left behind,
Again our ancient games had place,
The mimic picture's breathing grace,
And dance and song and hoodman-blind.

Who show'd a token of distress?
No single tear, no mark of pain:
O sorrow, then can sorrow wane?
O grief, can grief be changed to less?

O last regret, regret can die!
No – mixt with all this mystic frame,
Her deep relations are the same,
But with long use her tears are dry.

Christmas Thoughts, by a Modern Thinker

(after Mr Matthew Arnold)
W.H. Mallock

*One of the lesser-known English writers of the time was
William Hurrell Mallock (1849–1923), a political philosopher,
satirist and poet. These verses, which mix traditional festive
images and mournful introspection in almost equal measure,
come from his second collection of poems, published
in 1893.*

The windows of the church are bright;
'Tis Christmas Eve, a low wind breathes;
And girls with happy eyes to-night
Are hanging up the Christmas wreaths;

And village voices by-and-by
Will reach my windows through the trees,
With wild, sweet music: 'Praise on high
To God: on earth, good-will and peace.'

Oh, happy girls, that hang the wreaths!
Oh, village fiddlers, happy ye!
Christmas to you still truly breathes
Good-will and peace; but not to me.

Yes, gladness is your simple role,
Ye foolish girls, ye labouring poor;
But joy would ill beseem my soul –
To sigh, my part is, and endure

For once as Rousseau stood, I stand
Apart, made picturesque by grief –
One of a small world-weary band,
The orphans of a dead belief.

Through graveyards lone we love to stray,
And sadly the sad tombs explore,
And contradict the texts which say
That we shall rise once more.

Our faith is dead, of course; and grief
Fills its room up; and Christmas pie
And turkey cannot bring relief
To such as Obermann and I.

Ah, Obermann, and might I pass
This English Christmas-tide with thee,
Far by those inland waves whose glass
Brightens and breaks by Meillerie;

Or else amongst the sternest dells
Alp shags with pine, we'd mix our sighs,
Mourn at the sound of Christmas bells,
Sniff at the smell of Christmas pies.

But thou art dead; and long, dank grass
And wet mould cool thy tired, hot brain;
Thou art lain down, and now, alas!
Of course you won't get up again.

Yet, Obermann, 'tis better so;
For if, sad slumberer, after all
You were to re-arise, you know
'Twould make us feel so very small.

Best bear our grief this manlier way,
And make our grief be balm to grief;
For if in faith sweet comfort lay,
There lurks sweet pride in unbelief.

Wherefore, remembering this, once more
Unto my childhood's church I'll go,
And bow my head at that low door
I passed through standing, long ago.

I'll sit in the accustomed place,
And make, while all the unlearnèd stare,
A mournful, atheistic face
At their vain noise of unheard prayer.

Then, while they hymn the heavenly birth
And angel voices from the skies,
My thoughts shall go where Weimar's earth
For ever darkens Goethe's eyes;

Till sweet girls' glances from their books
Shall steal towards me, and they sigh:
'How intellectual he looks,
And yet how wistful! And his eye

Has that vain look of baffled prayer!'
And then when church is o'er I'll run,
Comb misery into all my hair,
And go and get my portrait done.

Reginald's Christmas Revel

Saki

The final years of Gilbert's writing career coincided with the rise of another master of black humour, the political journalist turned short story writer Saki (Hector Hugh Munro), 1870–1916. This suggestion for how to liven up what threatens to be an utterly tedious season of peace and goodwill comes from one of his earliest volumes, Reginald *(1904).*

They say (said Reginald) that there's nothing sadder than victory except defeat. If you've ever stayed with dull people during what is alleged to be the festive season, you can probably revise that saying. I shall never forget putting in a Christmas at the Babwolds'. Mrs. Babwold is some relation of my father's – a sort of to-be-left-till-called-for cousin – and that was considered sufficient reason for my having to accept her invitation at about the sixth time of asking; though why the sins of the father should be visited by the children – you won't find any notepaper in that drawer; that's where I keep old menus and first-night programmes.

Mrs. Babwold wears a rather solemn personality, and has never been known to smile, even when saying disagreeable things to her friends or making out the Stores list. She takes her pleasures sadly. A state elephant at a Durbar gives one a very similar impression. Her husband gardens in all weathers. When a man goes out in the pouring rain to brush caterpillars off rose trees, I generally imagine his life indoors leaves something to be desired; anyway, it must be very unsettling for the caterpillars.

Of course there were other people there. There was a Major Somebody who had shot things in Lapland, or somewhere of that sort; I forget what they were, but it wasn't for want of reminding. We had them cold with every meal almost, and he was continually giving us details of what they measured from tip to tip, as though he thought we were going to make them warm underthings for the winter. I used to listen to him with a rapt attention that I thought rather suited me, and then one day I quite modestly gave the dimensions of an okapi I had shot in the Lincolnshire fens. The Major turned a beautiful Tyrian scarlet (I remember thinking at the time that I should like my bathroom hung in that colour), and I think that at that moment he almost found it in his heart to dislike me. Mrs. Babwold put on a first-aid-to-the-injured expression, and asked him why he didn't publish a book of his sporting reminiscences; it would be so interesting. She didn't remember till afterwards that he had given her two fat volumes on the subject, with his portrait and autograph as a frontispiece and an appendix on the habits of the Arctic mussel.

It was in the evening that we cast aside the cares and distractions of the day and really lived. Cards were thought to be too frivolous and empty a way of passing the time, so most of them played what they called a book game. You went out into the hall – to get an inspiration, I suppose – then you came in again with a muffler tied round your neck and looked silly, and the others were supposed to guess that you were 'Wee MacGreegor.' I held out against the inanity as long as I decently could, but at last, in a lapse of good-nature, I consented to masquerade as a book, only I warned them that it would take some time to carry out. They waited for the best part of forty minutes while I went and played wineglass skittles with the page-boy in the pantry; you play it with a champagne cork, you know, and the one who knocks down the most glasses without breaking them wins. I won, with four unbroken out of seven; I think William suffered from over-anxiousness. They were rather mad in the drawing-room at my not having come back, and they weren't a bit pacified when I told them afterwards that I was 'At the end of the passage.'

'I never did like Kipling,' was Mrs. Babwold's comment, when the situation dawned upon her. 'I couldn't see anything clever in Earthworms out of Tuscany – or is that by Darwin?'

Of course these games are very educational, but, personally, I prefer bridge.

On Christmas evening we were supposed to be specially festive in the Old English fashion. The hall was horribly draughty, but it seemed to be the proper place to revel in, and it was decorated with Japanese fans and Chinese lanterns, which gave it a very Old English effect. A young lady with a confidential voice favoured us with a long recitation about a little girl who died or did something equally hackneyed, and then the Major gave us a graphic account of a struggle he had with a wounded bear. I privately wished that the bears would win sometimes on these occasions; at least they wouldn't go vapouring about it afterwards. Before we had time to recover our spirits, we were indulged with some thought-reading by a young man whom one knew instinctively had a good mother and an indifferent tailor – the sort of young man who talks unflaggingly through the thickest soup, and smooths his hair dubiously as though he thought it might hit back. The thought-reading was rather a success; he announced that the hostess was thinking about poetry, and she admitted that her mind was dwelling on one of Austin's odes. Which was near enough. I fancy she had been really wondering whether a scrag-end of mutton and some cold plum-pudding would do for the kitchen dinner next day. As a crowning dissipation, they all sat down to play progressive halma, with milk-chocolate for prizes. I've been carefully brought up, and I don't like to play games of skill for milk-chocolate, so I invented a headache and retired from the scene. I had been preceded a few minutes earlier by Miss Langshan-Smith, a rather formidable lady, who always got up at some uncomfortable hour in the morning, and gave you the impression that she had been in communication with most of the European Governments before breakfast. There was a paper pinned on her door with a signed request that she might be called particularly early on the morrow. Such an opportunity does not come twice in a lifetime. I covered up everything except the signature with another notice, to the effect that before these words should meet the eye she would have ended a misspent life, was sorry for the trouble she was giving, and would like a military funeral. A few minutes later I violently exploded an air-filled paper bag on the landing, and gave a stage moan that could have been heard in the cellars. Then I pursued my original intention and went to bed. The noise those people made in forcing open the good lady's door was positively indecorous; she resisted gallantly, but I believe they searched for bullets for about a quarter of an hour, as if she had been a historic battlefield.

I hate travelling on Boxing Day, but one must occasionally do things that one dislikes.

Gilbert at Christmas

Kate Terry Gielgud

In Kate Terry Gielgud: An Autobiography *(1953), the actress and mother of Sir John Gielgud described some of the seasonal entertainments the librettist and his wife devised for her and her siblings at their successive homes in Kensington, at The Boltons and Harrington Gardens. Born in July 1868, Kate would have been aged between about ten and fourteen at the time she describes.*

In striking contrast to the grandeur and vastness of Covent Garden was a rather dingy little playhouse in the Strand – the Opéra Comique, where in 1878 *H.M.S. Pinafore* was produced, written by W.S. Gilbert, with music by Arthur Sullivan. Both author and composer were friends of my parents, and Mr. and Mrs. Gilbert invited us every year to Christmas parties in their house in The Boltons. As he bade us good-night Mr. Gilbert would ask if we would like to come to the theatre. He insisted that we should, in that case, write him a letter; we always received a prompt reply from him, enclosing tickets for dress circle or for a box. The first time it was for a matinée on 20th March, 1880, when we saw *H.M.S. Pinafore* acted by children – 'professional children' – among them Harry and Emilie Grattan, son and daughter of H. Plunkett Grattan.

H.M.S. Pinafore was the first I saw of that series of musical comedies which seem to make an ageless appeal,

Kate Terry Gielgud, 1883 (By kind permission of Mander & Mitchenson Theatre Collection)

Rutland Barrington, always the
'portly big man'

and are still popular all over the world. *The Pirates of Penzance* followed in the same year, and *Patience* in 1881 – all at the Opéra Comique. Meanwhile the Savoy Theatre was being built by Mr. D'Oyly Carte with a new lighting system – electricity! At the same time the Gilberts built a new house in Harrington Gardens with a model of H.M.S. *Pinafore* as a weather-vane, and this house too had electric light installed in it, and here the Christmas tree, instead of being hung with candles and parcels, was a dazzling mass of tiny festooned globes, blue, red, green and yellow, a light within each. Parcels were heaped on the floor so as not to spoil the effect, but were disregarded in the clamour to be allowed to move the switch in the wall that could plunge the room into darkness and, reversed, restore the light in a dozen fittings at once. We gaped in wonder, and in 1882 at the Savoy, when we saw *Iolanthe*, each fairy carried a wand star-tipped with an electric light and wore another in her hair. We went behind the scenes and were shown the little batteries and switches concealed in the fluffy dresses to make the 'will-o' the-wisp' effects we had marvelled at. There, and at the parties, we met members of the company, and already I was deeply interested in the contrasted performances of these people each successive year – their change from the lackadaisical aesthetes of *Patience* to the hearty, heavily-robed Peers, from the swooning ladies in their 'greenery-yallery' draperies to the tripping fairies – and the even greater contrast when *The Mikado* gave to them all the slanting eyes, black hair, and exquisite kimonos of Japan.

There was always a family likeness about these plays: always the portly big man – Rutland Barrington – and the tiny, dapper George Grossmith, so light on his feet and so nimble of tongue; the massive (or angular) spinster to set off the dainty fragility of Jessie Bond; in each play were

Detail from an autograph letter from Gilbert to Miss Terry, 20 December 1876:
'Wishing you both a decent, sober, temperate & respectable Christmas,
undisfigured by extravagance & untainted by excess. I am, Very Truly Yours,
WS Gilbert'. (By kind permission of the Pierpont Morgan Library, Gilbert and
Sullivan Collection, New York)

courtships and contretemps, love songs, patter songs, choruses, imposing or truculent, the final pairings off – endless variety, but easily followed even by small people because of just this underlying familiarity, and the tunes that one could hum (or rather, my sisters could) and to which we loved to dance.

The Beauty Stone

A.W. Pinero and J.W.C. Carr

The Beauty Stone *was one of the last of Sullivan's collaborations, his librettists being Arthur Wing Pinero (1855–1934) and Joseph William Comyns Carr (1849-1916). This 'original romantic musical drama in three acts' told the story of an ugly, disfigured peasant girl transformed by a magic 'beauty stone' to win the heart of a dashing hero. Its effects soon wear off, the hero is blinded in battle, and they live happily ever after (romantically at least), the hero unaware of his bride's bad looks having returned. Opening at the Savoy Theatre in May 1898, its solemn flavour was more suited to Covent Garden where audiences, not expecting comedy, might have more readily accepted a production lasting over four hours on its opening night. It ran for only 50 performances, a failure by Sullivan's standards, but one he may have expected. Pinero and Carr, he said, were 'gifted and brilliant men, with no experience in writing for music'. These two fragments from the closing act, from songs addressed by Lord Philip of Mirlemont (the hero) to Laine (the heroine), use winter and snow as charming romantic images.*

And what if it be true
That her eyes are softest blue,
And her lips like winter berries
Shyly peeping through the snow,
That she wears a smaller shoe
Than some other maidens do?
Yet for all she is not fairest;
Therefore, prithee, let her go.
If the cloak of winter be naught
But the glittering garment of spring;
If the whispering silence of night
But tells of the dawn that is there;
Then the veil on these eyes is no more
Than a shadow that falls from Love's wing,
'Tis love that proclaims thee to-day
The fairest of all that are fair.

The Last Night of the Year

H.F. Chorley

Sullivan composed music for many part songs as well as hymns and Christmas carols. The words to this song, published in 1873, were written by Henry Fothergill Chorley (1808–72), author of novels, drama and verse, and musical editor of the weekly Athenaeum. *The two also collaborated on an opera,* The Sapphire Necklace, *written 1863–4 but never produced, and the original score was lost. An overture and two excerpts were produced at the Crystal Palace in 1867 under a new title,* The False Heiress.

The good old year's a-waning,
The good old year's a-waning;
He brought us care and woe,
But we'll forgive the wrong he wrought,
   the wrong he wrought,
But we'll forgive the wrong he wrought,
Before we let him go,
We will not look around us
For those who once were here,
But count the good that's left us still,
On the last night of the year,
But count the good that's left us still,
On the last night of the year.

He carried off their riches
From some in springtime proud,

But summer's heavy hearted ones
He made to laugh aloud,
But summer's heavy hearted ones
He made to laugh aloud;
And though his months went over
With many a sigh and tear,
We will not stay to tell them now,
On the last night of the year,
We will not stay to tell them now,
On the last night of the year.

He broke full many a friendship,
And many a lover's vow!
But he hath let us meet again,
So we'll not blame him now,
But he hath let us meet again,
So we'll not blame him now,
Nor look behind nor forward,
In sorrow or with fear,
But send the cup of hope about
On the last night of the year,
But send the cup of hope about
On the last night of the year.

The typical 'Victorian' Christmas scene soon caught on throughout Europe, as this French card shows.

Acknowledgements

Thanks are due to the Random House Group Ltd for permission to quote from *Secrets of a Savoyard*, by Henry A. Lytton, originally published by Jarrold, and *Here's a how-de-do*, Martyn Green, originally published by Max Reinhardt; to Bodley Head for permission to quote from *An autobiography*, by Kate Terry Gielgud; and to Simon & Schuster for permission to quote from *The story of my life*, by Queen Marie of Roumania, originally published by Cassell & Co. The vast majority of prose, verse and illustrations used is in the public domain. Every effort has been made to trace and contact the original owners of remaining material, but in a few cases this has not been possible. If any such owners or originators have not been acknowledged, please write to the compiler c/o the publisher.

In addition, particular thanks are due to Stephen Turnbull of the Sir Arthur Sullivan Society, Chris Browne, John Cannon, David Cookson, Andrew Crowther, Peter Joslin, and Melvyn Tarran, for general advice and the supply or loan of various out-of-copyright material, both text and illustrations. I contacted some of these gentlemen through the Gilbert & Sullivan Archive on the Internet, a breathtaking resource which is so shamelessly addictive that it should really carry some kind of health warning. Also, my editors at Sutton

Publishing: Jaqueline Mitchell, Anne Bennett and Kate Bennett.

Among the books to which I am indebted for much of my background information, I would like to acknowledge and recommend particularly the following: *Gilbert, A Victorian and his Theatre*, by Jane Stedman (Oxford University Press 1996); *Sir Arthur Sullivan, a Victorian musician*, by Arthur Jacobs (Oxford University Press 1984), *Gilbert and Sullivan*, by Alan James (Omnibus Press 1989), and that lively if occasionally inaccurate hardy perennial, *Gilbert and Sullivan* by Hesketh Pearson (Hamish Hamilton 1935, often reprinted).

In conclusion I would like to dedicate this anthology to my mother, Mrs Kate Van der Kiste, and my aunt, Mrs Jill Monk, whose parents were both leading lights of the Gilbert & Sullivan Amateur Operatic Society of Aylsham, Norfolk, between the wars, and thanks to whom I was introduced to the Savoy Operas, on record and on stage, in early childhood.

Also in the Sutton Publishing Christmas series:

THE GREAT BRITISH CHRISTMAS
Edited by Maria Hubert

A COUNTRY HOUSE CHRISTMAS
Edited by John Chandler
(In association with the National Trust)